Christ
Is
Everything

H.G. Souza

CHRIST IS EVERYTHING
The Mystery of God's Will is to Sum Up All Things in Christ
Copyright © 2026 by H.G. Souza

ISBN: 979-8-9946034-0-6

Library of Congress Control Number: 2026904709

Disclaimer:
This book is based on the author's personal spiritual journey, study, and understanding of the Holy Scriptures. It is provided for informational and inspirational purposes only.

Unless otherwise indicated, all Scripture quotations are from The Holy Bible, American Standard Version (New York: Thomas Nelson, 1901). All rights reserved.

Printed in the United States of America

Table of Contents

Endorsement

Christ is Everything is a book that empowers you to step into a realignment of vision, identity, and hope. This is not an invitation to try harder at Christianity; it is an invitation to see more clearly the One who already holds your life together. Helber carries a simple yet life-altering message: God has one plan for your life, one source for your growth, and one answer for every lack—and His name is Jesus. This book prophetically calls you back to the truth that Christ is not just your Savior—He is your life.

As you read, expect the Holy Spirit to lift your eyes from what you think you lack and anchor you in what you already have. Patience, humility, love, and strength are not distant goals you must achieve; they are the natural fruit of abiding in Christ. The cross is not merely a past event—it is a present reality declaring that your identity is secure, your future is settled, and your transformation is inevitable. This book releases hope because it removes pressure. It reminds you that growth does not come from self-effort, but from union; not from fixing yourself, but from trusting the finished work of Jesus. You are not missing something—you are discovering Someone. And as Christ is revealed more fully to you, freedom will follow naturally.

I believe Christ Is Everything will awaken joy, restore confidence, and renew vision in your heart. May this book strengthen your faith, quiet striving, and cause you declare to yourself: "The best days of my life are ahead!"

Steve Backlund - Igniting Hope Ministries

Introduction

Let me share a little bit about how God came to me for the long run, not just for the moment. I was raised in a Christian family, so I heard. My introduction to Christian life was based on a childhood routine. My earliest memories of that involve attending church mass with my mother every Sunday at 7 AM, followed by a visit to the farmers market for groceries. For years, this was the Sunday morning schedule. My understanding of God was limited to the message that He sent Jesus, His son, to save us. The concept of being '**saved**' remained undefined.

Around the age of ten, I observed a different role for God. My mother referred to Him as the solution for problems that appeared to have no practical answer. During this period, my parents' faith seemed private, expressed through quiet prayers in their room to a seemingly distant God. The regularity of our attendance at Sunday mass decreased, and I only heard God's name being mentioned by my parents. The established ritual of faith began to diminish.

Adolescence, at fifteen, introduced the idea of God as a last resort during times of difficulty. My involvement in early employment, new friendships, and changes in appearance—while not truly rebellious—caused a noticeable shift. My father decided on an intervention, purchasing a Bible, and proposing we read it together. Prior to this, I have no recollection of ever interacting with a physical Bible.

The initial experience of reading the Bible with my father was challenging. We read only a few pages, and neither of us seemed to grasp the full context. I felt a clear resistance to that practice. However, I observed that my father continued to read independently of me. This shared Bible reading attempt, combined with the earlier memory of my mother's private prayers, established a foundational sense: the observation that God was real, a presence that existed regardless of my ability to perceive or comprehend it.

The realization culminated at age eighteen: I concluded that God was **pursuing** me. This was not a response to a consciously perceived crisis; deep inside I was desperate for Jesus and didn't know it. My real Christian life commenced with this recognition of His presence. I began to see that He had been consistently present, waiting for me to acknowledge Him, waiting for me to embrace His work at the cross.

The main takeaway is this: God is with me for the long run, not just for the momentary fix. The work of the cross in my life is not a historical event, it is a daily event. God's plan for me is to sum up "all things" in Christ, and I mean "everything", whether I understand it or not. This is not a historical event either, but it is His daily work in me. To me there is no Christian life apart from Christ and the continuous work of the cross.

It is at the cross that Christ says, "it is finished", and it is there where He says it is finished that my real life starts and ends.

1

Nothing But Christ

If you picked this book to read it is because, whether you know it or not, you have an inner desire for Christ, and the good news is, whether you know it or not, that Christ also has an inner desire for you. God the Father has one plan for life, any kind of life, and His plan is the Son. Sounds simplistic, but yes, it is that simple. The mystery of God's will is to sum up "all things" in Christ. The Christian life, as the name suggests, is a life in Christ. Let's see how Romans 11:36 explains the dynamics of the Christian life "For from Him and through Him and to Him are all things". So, it is quite simple, for us life comes from Christ, we live it through Christ, and our greatest goal is also Christ himself.

> The mystery of God's will is to sum up all things in Christ.
> (Ephesians 1:9-10 ASV)

Our Security, Our Source, Our Everything

Jesus told them, "When you lift up the Son of Man, then **you**

will truly know who I am" (John 8:28). This is a profound and encouraging promise! Jesus is letting us know that His ultimate sacrifice—His pivotal work on the cross, the moment He was 'lifted up'—is the key to unlocking the deepest revelation of His true identity. When we look to the cross, we don't just see a historical event; we see the very heart of God's love and saving grace. In that glorious moment, we discover the complete truth that He is indeed our Savior, our Lord, and the answer to every need.

The wonderful truth is that you have already died to your old life, and your new, real life is hidden securely **with Christ in God.** (Romans 6:4-8). And when **Christ—who is our life— is revealed in glory, you will be revealed with Him in that same glory!** (Colossians 3:3-4). What an incredible security and future we have! This isn't just about a distant promise; it's a profound, present reality. Because you are united with Christ, your true self is untouchable, hidden in the most secure place in the universe. Right now, Christ *is* your life—the very source of your strength, joy, and purpose. One day, when He shines forth in His full glory, you will shine right along with Him! Until then, live each day confidently, knowing your identity is safe and sealed in Him.

The wonderful truth is that you have already died to your old life, and your new, real life is hidden securely with Christ in God. And when Christ—who is our life—is revealed in glory, you will be revealed with Him in that same glory!

Think about this magnificent truth: Everything—absolutely everything—was created in Him, through Him, and for Him. This includes all of existence, visible and invisible, from powerful rulers to celestial beings. He was there before anything else, and the entire universe holds together because of Him. He is the head of the church, which is His body. He is the beginning, the very first to be raised from the dead, so that in **everything** **He** might have the place of honor and preeminence. God was pleased to let all of His divine fullness dwell in Christ, and through Him, God has reconciled the entire universe back to Himself, making peace through the blood of His cross—peace with everything on earth and in heaven (Colossians 1:16-20). This passage paints the most stunning portrait of Jesus Christ! It means He isn't just a part of your life; He is the divine blueprint for all life, the glue that keeps your world from falling apart, and the ultimate purpose of all creation. This truth empowers us! You are connected to the One who is the source of all power, all glory, and all life. Because of His finished work on the cross, the conflict between God and humanity is over, and you are reconciled to God and living in a state of eternal peace. He is the *All in All*, and you are wonderfully *in Him*.

The Transformative Gift: Moving Beyond a "Checklist" Christianity

The single, magnificent gift we receive from God is His Son, Jesus Christ. Yet, as believers, our understanding of this central truth often varies dramatically. Some see Jesus as one significant gift among a vast collection of spiritual blessings, while others have grasped the glorious reality that He is God's *only* all-encompassing gift. We may initially receive Christ as the "first" gift—the one that saves us—but mistakenly assume that thousands of other, lesser gifts and virtues must be acquired separately over time. A deeper, more liberating confession, however, is that Jesus Christ is not just *a* gift; He is the *total* Gift, the sole provision of God for every aspect of our lives. This profound difference in perspective is the key to unlocking a truly victorious and restful Christian life.

It can be truly surprising when we begin our journey with Christ and quickly discover that being "saved" doesn't instantly erase all of our deep-seated flaws and struggles. We might find that a quick, frustrating temper still flares up, pride still subtly directs our decisions, or that an old, paralyzing lack of hope still grips our hearts. We become new Christians, yes, but we are new Christians with noticeable character deficiencies. Our immediate, natural response to these imperfections is to strive to fix them.

In this stage of the Christian experience, it's common to find ourselves praying for, expecting, and diligently seeking numerous individual "gifts" to fill these perceived gaps. We sincerely pray for patience, ask for an increase of humility, and desperately try to cultivate more love. We naturally count Christ among these gifts—the most important one, of course— but still just one item on a long spiritual shopping list. When we feel like we've successfully overcome a specific deficiency— finally controlling that temper or overcoming a moment of pride—our heart genuinely rejoices over what we perceive as a successful acquisition, a new "gift" obtained from God's hand.

The "Fill-in-the-Blanks" Mentality

In this common yet incomplete understanding, many believers view God's grace as a spiritual "patch kit"—a divine supply designed merely to replenish their individual lacks or "wants." In this mindset, the Christian life becomes a kind of fill-in-the-blanks test. We might think, "What else is God's grace for, if not to fill up my missing qualities?" We see ourselves as fundamentally good, but just missing a few pieces for completion. "My love is almost perfect," one might think, "but it would be even better if I could just add a little humility and a dash of patience. Once these supplements are added, then I'll be complete, I'll be a mature Christian." This human concept is deeply rooted in our sense of lack, and as a result, we constantly petition God for the specific, countable supplies we believe we need.

We frame our requests for these virtues as distinct "things" or "objects" we are missing. We look around at others, measuring our needs against their apparent strengths: "I wish I wasn't so quick-tempered; look how patient Mr. So-and-So is! I wish I wasn't so proud; look how gentle and humble that woman is." It is incredibly difficult to pray for something we have not yet seen, so we often end up praying for a measure of humility or patience that resembles what another person exhibits. This external focus on a visible trait that someone else possesses is the core of the problem.

Everything good, true, and virtuous flows only from Christ. The Christian journey is not a quest for a collection of spiritual traits; it is a deepening, intimate relationship with the One Person in whom all virtues perfectly reside.

Imagine this: if God were to instantly take the patience of another person and "deposit" it within you, would you be satisfied? Most likely, your answer would be a joyful *yes*! This deep desire stems from the fact that we often see spiritual virtues—like patience—as a separate, measurable *thing* that others possess and that we, sadly, do not. We may struggle with deep self-criticism, hating ourselves for our temper, and wishing we could just acquire that virtue. Consequently, many in the church long for a specific item—a controlled temper, a quiet spirit—which they believe is a virtue God possesses and has bestowed upon certain spiritual people, but which they are missing. Their pressing need, as they see it, is simply to have that "thing" added to them so they can be patient and complete people too.

The Core Difference: Christ vs. Concepts

This is the candid and profound point of divergence between a vibrant, living, authentic Christianity and one that is faulty or merely theoretical. Many sincere believers are constantly looking for something—a virtue, a trait, a spiritual quality—that seems to be everywhere *except* in their own lives. They observe it in other people, yet they don't possess it themselves. Thus, their entire spiritual focus becomes a quest for a separate, tangible *thing* that they can pursue, possess, and then celebrate once it's acquired. They pursue the item, they get the item, and they rejoice over the obtained gift.

The glorious, liberating truth that the Holy Spirit wants to reveal to us is this: **In the spiritual realm, there is no "thing" apart from Christ.** There is no such separate object called "patience," or "humility," or "light" that exists independently. **There is only Christ, and Him alone.** Everything good, true, and virtuous flows only from His Person. The Christian journey is not a quest for a collection of spiritual traits; it is a deepening, intimate relationship with the One Person in whom all virtues perfectly reside. It is a shift from striving to *have* a thing to simply abiding *in* the Person.

Heavenly Father, we come to you with hearts full of thanksgiving for the profound mystery and simplicity of your will to sum up all things in Christ.

Thank you for the glorious truth that Christ is not merely a gift, but your *total* and *only* Gift—the sole provision for every aspect of our lives. We are grateful that our journey is not a striving to acquire virtues, but a restful, intimate relationship with the living Person of Jesus Christ, in whom all virtues perfectly reside.

We thank you, Lord, that in the spiritual realm, there is no "thing" apart from Christ, for He is the essence of all good, true, and virtuous reality. We praise you that our old life is truly dead, and our new, real life is hidden securely with Christ in God. What incredible security and future we have!

May we live each day confidently, resting in the liberating truth that Christ is our life, our source, and our everything. May our focus forever be shifted from a religious mindset to simply abiding in Him.

In the mighty name of Jesus, our All in All, we pray. Amen.

2

Christ is God's Everything

The next day he saw Jesus coming to him and said, "Look! The Lamb of God [a]who takes away the sin of the world!" (John 1:29 AMP)

Jesus replied to them, "I am the Bread of Life. The one who comes to Me will never be hungry, and the one who believes in Me \[as Savior\] will never be thirsty \[for that one will be sustained spiritually\]." (John 6:35 AMP)

And Jesus said to them, "I assure you and most solemnly say to you, unless you eat the flesh of the Son of Man and drink His blood \[unless you believe in Me as Savior and believe in the saving power of My blood which will be shed for you\], you do not have life in yourselves." (John 6:53 AMP)

Once more Jesus addressed the crowd. He said, "I am the Light of the world. He who follows Me will not walk in the darkness, but will have the Light of life." (John 8:12 AMP)

"That is why I told you that you will die \[unforgiven and

condemned\] in your sins; for if you do not believe that I am the One \[I claim to be\], you will die in your sins." (John 8:24 AMP)

Jesus said to her, "I am \[Myself\] the Resurrection and the Life. Whoever believes in (adheres to, trusts in, and relies on) Me, although he may die, yet he shall live." (John 11:25 AMPC) So Jesus said, "When you lift up the Son of Man \[on the cross\], you will know then \[without any doubt\] that I am He, and that I do nothing on My own authority, but I say these things just as My Father taught Me." (John 8:28 AMP)

Jesus said to him, "I am the \[only\] Way \[to God\] and the \[real\] Truth and the \[real\] Life; no one comes to the Father but through Me." (John 14:6 AMP)

But it is from Him that you are in Christ Jesus, who became to us wisdom from God \[revealing His plan of salvation\], and righteousness \[making us acceptable to God\], and sanctification \[making us holy and setting us apart for God\], and redemption \[providing our ransom from the penalty for sin\]. (1 Corinthians 1:30 AMP)

When Christ, Who is our life, appears, then you also will appear with Him in \[the splendor of His\] glory. (Colossians 3:4 AMPC)

Paul, an apostle (special messenger, personally chosen representative) of Christ Jesus by the commandment of God our Savior, and of Christ Jesus (the Messiah, the Anointed) our Hope \[the fulfillment of our salvation\]. (1 Timothy 1:1 AMP)

The LORD is my light and my salvation— Whom shall I fear? The LORD is the refuge and fortress of my life— Whom shall I dread? (Psalm 27:1 AMP)

Christ: The Divine Purpose For Us and Our Empowering Journey To Him

In the grand tapestry of God's eternal plan, Christ stands as both the ultimate destination and the very path that leads us there. It's a beautiful journey that begins with Christ, happens through Christ, and culminates in Christ. To truly grasp the depth of God's magnificent purpose, we can turn to the profound insights found in the books of Ephesians and Colossians, which illuminate this divine truth.

Ephesians beautifully reveals how, according to God's intentional and loving design, He has orchestrated all of history to converge and find its glorious fulfillment in Christ. Imagine a cosmic symphony where every note, every instrument, every movement, is perfectly harmonized to bring everything—both in the heavens above and on the earth below—into a magnificent unity centered on Jesus. It's a breathtaking vision of all creation finding its true meaning and purpose in Him.

Colossians takes this revelation even further, showing us that Christ isn't just a central figure; He is absolutely preeminent in every single aspect of existence. More than that, He is to be *all* and *in all*. This means Christ isn't merely the goal we're striving for; He is also the very power, the very presence, and the very essence that enables us to reach that goal. He is the means by which God's grand design unfolds. For God's deepest desire is for Christ to hold the supreme position in everything. To achieve this, Christ *must* be everything. It's only through His all-encompassing nature, His dwelling within all things, that He can truly bring everything together—both celestial and earthly—into perfect alignment. If Christ is truly all, then it's a natural consequence that all things find their complete summation in Him. If He lives and breathes in all, what else could possibly define existence?

> Christ is absolutely preeminent in every single aspect of existence. More than that, He is to be all and in all. This means Christ isn't merely the goal we're striving for; He is also the very power, the very presence, and the very essence that enables us to reach that goal.

It's a liberating truth to remember that in God's eyes, there is only Christ, not a multitude of separate "things" or "affairs." He doesn't see isolated events or disconnected matters; His gaze is solely fixed on Christ. The complexities and concerns that often preoccupy our human minds—the endless "affairs" and "things" we perceive in the world today—are, from God's eternal perspective, simply non-existent apart from Christ. Our worldly viewpoint might categorize countless issues and matters, but according to God's infinite wisdom, Christ is all-encompassing. Consequently, there are no truly separate affairs or things; Christ *is* all, and He is *in* all. And this glorious reality is precisely when God's eternal purpose will be fully and magnificently realized.

Embrace this incredible truth: Christ will lovingly and powerfully bring all things into perfect unity within Himself. This isn't a distant future hope; it's a beautiful work that has already begun and is actively unfolding within the church today. It's not something that will only start in a future age, nor will it only become true when God's eternal purpose reaches its final culmination.

God, in His boundless grace, is actively opening our spiritual eyes right now to see that within the church, Christ is both the very essence of our spiritual endeavors and the substance of all true spiritual realities. The church is beginning to awaken to this profound understanding, and as we do, we commence living in this vibrant spiritual world. If the church continues to perceive a separation between "things" and "affairs" and Christ, it simply indicates that we haven't yet fully grasped the glorious vision of Christ as all. And of course, the "things" and "affairs" we speak of here aren't just the mundane matters of this world; they point especially to the profound spiritual matters and divine affairs that truly define our existence in Him.

It's quite striking how John's Gospel includes so many unique insights and narratives not found in the other biblical accounts of Jesus' life. This Gospel, considered the most profound and the last to be written among them, emerged after the entire New Testament had already taken shape, following the other Gospels and numerous Epistles. John's contribution, therefore, serves as a culminating revelation, offering us a profound glimpse into God's ultimate estimation of Christ and guiding us on how we, too, can come to know Christ in the same intimate way God knows Him.

Through John's inspired writing, we come to a deeper understanding that God's ultimate desire isn't merely for a sacrificial lamb, nor is what He provides simply "the bread of life" as an external offering. We also learn that God doesn't just *supply* the way, the truth, and the life as separate concepts, nor does Christ simply *use* His power to restore human life or sight. Instead, the overwhelming and singular truth woven throughout John's Gospel is that Christ *is* all these things.

When Jesus declares, "I am the light of the world," He isn't saying He *can give* people light; He's asserting that He *is* the very source and essence of light itself. Similarly, when

He states, "I am the bread of life," He's not promising to *provide* us with bread; He's proclaiming that He *is* the life-sustaining nourishment our souls truly crave. He says, "I am the way," not that He will *guide* us along a path. He proclaims, "I am the truth," not that He will *teach* us a truth. And He affirms, "I am true life," not that He will *bestow* a life upon us. This profound distinction is powerfully illustrated when Lazarus died: Christ didn't tell Mary and Martha that He *had the power* to raise their brother; instead, He declared, "I am the resurrection." He is not just the one who *does* these things; He *is* the very embodiment of them.

It's crucial to grasp this fundamental principle: in Christianity, there are no mere "things" or abstract concepts separate from Christ. The "bread of life," the "light," the "way," the "truth," "life" itself, the "resurrection," or even "the lamb" – these are not independent entities. No, the core of the matter is that there is *only Christ*! What we truly need to comprehend in our walk with God is that our spiritual experience isn't about acquiring a collection of spiritual "things" or engaging in a series of "affairs." It's solely about Christ Himself. It's not that He *gives* us light, but that He *is* our light. It's not that He *leads* the way, but He *is* the way. It's not that He *grants* us a life, but He *is* our life. It's not that He *imparts* a truth, but He *is* the truth. Do you perceive the profound difference here? Every single thing Christ give is, in reality, His very own self, extended to us in love and grace.

Discovering the Christ of John's Gospel

It's truly fascinating to see how the Gospel of John stands out from the rest. It wasn't just another historical account; it was penned last, offering a deep, spiritual perspective that beautifully completes the New Testament narrative. John's writing is profoundly focused, going beyond the daily ministry to show us God's ultimate view of His Son—and how we, too, can come to know Christ in the most intimate, life-changing way. It's an invitation to move from simple belief to radical, transforming encounter.

What we uncover in John's message is a powerful shift in perspective. It challenges the traditional idea that God simply provides spiritual items or services for us to use. It's not that God offers us a sacrificial lamb in the abstract, or hands us a piece of "bread of life," or gives us a spiritual road map to follow. John makes it crystal clear: Jesus doesn't merely use His power to give life, light, or truth; He is the very essence of all these things.

This realization is the monumental, central fact of John's Gospel—Christ is the comprehensive reality that underpins our entire faith. When He says, "I am the light of the world," He isn't saying, "I'm able to give you light." When He declares, "I am the bread of life," He isn't promising to just supply spiritual food. He doesn't offer to guide us to the Way; He is the Way we walk. He doesn't teach us a truth; He is the living embodiment of all Truth. And in the face of death, He didn't just assure Mary and Martha, "I have the power to raise your brother." Instead, in the most profound declaration of His very being, He said, "I am the resurrection."

This is an immensely liberating truth for us today: In Christianity, the focus is never on external "things," but solely on the living Person of Christ!

Think of the "things" we often pursue: light, guidance, spiritual life, truth, power, resurrection. These are wonderful concepts, but the whole matter is this: in our actual experience with God, we don't receive mere things or religious affairs; we receive

Christ Himself. It's not that He gives us light, but that He is our Light that shines from within. It's not that He leads the way, but that He is the Way we inhabit. It's not that He hands us a life, but that He is our very Life source! He doesn't simply teach us truth; He is the Truth that sets us free.

Do you see the incredible difference here? This is not just a theological fine point; it is the key to an effortless, thriving spiritual life! Everything Christ gives is His very own self—His love, His nature, His victory, His peace.

The good news is that God's plan for your life is beautifully simple: Christ is God's everything, because God offers nothing less than His Son to you! He hasn't given you a set of rules or a fragmented list of blessings; He has given you Christ. He gives Christ to be your light, Christ to be your strength, Christ to be your daily sustenance, and Christ to be the glorious Way, the enduring Truth, and the abundant Life.

When your eyes are opened to this glorious fact, the pressure to do more, achieve more, or remember a complex method dissolves. Your spiritual journey is transformed from striving for a religious product into simply receiving and enjoying a relationship with the Person who is everything you will ever need. Look to Him today, for in Christ, you have all things.

How Paul and David saw the Christ

I want you to grasp a magnificent truth that the Apostle Paul understood deeply—a truth that aligns perfectly with what Jesus Himself declared. Paul knew the Lord intimately, and his letters unveil some profound, life-altering facts about what Christ means to us.

Christ is Our Hope - First, Paul tells Timothy that "Christ Jesus (who is) our hope." Doesn't that phrase just resonate with power? It's much more liberating than saying, "Our hope is in Christ." That little word "in" can imply we're pinning an expectation onto an external figure, waiting to be given hope by Him. But Paul says Christ Jesus is the hope. He is the living, breathing, unshakeable reality of our future, our security, and our confident expectation. It's not a thing He gives you to hold onto; it's Himself dwelling within you as the absolute guarantee of glory. Your hope isn't a feeling that fades; it's a Person who never fails.

Christ is Our Life - Then, in his letter to the Colossians, Paul delivers another masterpiece: "When Christ, who is our life, shall be manifested." Notice the profound simplicity: "Christ, who is our life." He doesn't say, "When the life Christ gives is revealed," but rather, "When Christ our life is revealed." This is a spiritual game-changer! It forces us to see that the whole of the Christian life is not about acquiring blessings or spiritual attributes, but about possessing one Person. Truly, a Christian possesses nothing but Christ—and in Him, we have everything. He isn't just the Giver of abundant life; He is the divine, effortless wellspring of life flowing through you every single moment.

Christ is Our Wisdom, Righteousness, Sanctification, and Redemption - Perhaps one of the most encouraging and central scriptures is 1 Corinthians 1:30, where Paul declares that God has placed us in Christ Jesus, who became for us wisdom from God—and righteousness, sanctification, and redemption. This powerful verse reveals the heart of God's plan. God hasn't handed us separate, divisible gifts or "things":

He hasn't just given us righteousness; He gives us Christ, who is our Righteousness.
He hasn't simply given us a process of sanctification; He gives

us Christ, who is our very Sanctification.

He hasn't merely given us an external act of redemption; He gives us Christ, who is our Redemption.

He hasn't simply given us knowledge; He gives us Christ, who is our Wisdom.

This is why we can boldly proclaim that God's Christ is God's everything. Aside from Him, God offers no other spiritual "package."

Take, for example, our justification. Paul doesn't say God made Jesus our "justifier" (though He is that too!). He says God made Jesus our justification. This is much more than a legal declaration; it's a personal reality. Jesus did not come to sanctify us and then leave us with a task to keep up; He came to be our Sanctification—a living, constant, and effortless work. Our sanctification is not a behavior, a set of actions, or a religious duty; it is a Person, Christ Himself, being lived out through us.

This beautiful and vital truth remains: Christ is not only our Redeemer but also our Redemption. He is not only our Sanctifier but also our Sanctification. He is not only our Justifier but also our Righteousness. He is not only the one who makes us wise but is Himself our Wisdom.

Thank God for this liberating message! When you truly grasp that Christ gives you Himself—that everything you need is embodied in Him—you can stop striving to achieve and simply start receiving and resting in the glorious Person of Jesus Christ. You have everything because you have Him.

Christ is Our Personal Salvation - When we talk about faith, it's automatic for us to say, "The Lord Jesus is our Savior." And that is absolutely true! He rescues us, delivers us, and redeems us. But let's pause and consider a deeper, even more profound truth revealed by King David in Psalm 27:1, where he declares, "The Lord... is my salvation."

It's not just that the Lord acts as our Savior; David saw that the Lord is the very state of being saved. Jesus is not just the one who saves you; He is the living, ultimate Salvation itself.

This revelation moves us from simply trusting His actions to embracing His very Person. The Lord Jesus holds both titles: He is our marvelous Savior, and He is the complete, glorious reality of our Salvation. This is the profound heart of God's gift to us. God doesn't hand out "salvation" as a separate spiritual commodity; He gives us the Lord Jesus Himself. In Him, the act of saving and the complete state of being saved become one, making your life in Christ whole, secure, and eternally abundant.

Christ is not only our Redeemer but also our Redemption. He is not only our Sanctifier but also our Sanctification. He is not only our Justifier but also our Righteousness. He is not only the one who makes us wise but is Himself our Wisdom.

Heavenly Father, I humble myself before you and surrender to the magnificent truth that Christ is your everything, and therefore, my everything.

I surrender my striving to acquire spiritual "things" or to perfect myself through a religious effort. I confess that I looked in the past for separated virtues, but your liberating truth shows me that there is no "thing" apart from Christ, for He is the essence of all I need.

I surrender my old understanding and embrace the profound reality of your Son. I receive Him now as the Bread of Life, the sustenance for my soul; the Light of my life, the truth that dispels all my darkness; the Way and the Method, the living path that leads to you, my very Life, my Hope, and the complete Resurrection of my life.

I rest in the truth that Christ is all and in all. I surrender my complexities and concerns, acknowledging that from your eternal perspective, Christ is the only affair. I cease from my own efforts and simply choose to abide in the living Person of Jesus Christ.

Let my life be a continual, joyful surrender to Christ, who is my Salvation, my Source, and the glorious destination of all your purposes.

In the mighty name of Jesus, my All in All, I pray. Amen.

3

Christ Is the Way, the Truth, and the Life

Jesus said to him, **I am the Way, and the Truth, and the Life;** no one comes to the Father except through Me. (John 14:6)

Discovering Our Everything in Christ

In a moment of profound revelation that echoes through eternity, Jesus declared to us, "**I am the Way, and the Truth, and the Life;** no one comes to the Father except through Me" (John 14:6). This isn't merely a statement, but a loving invitation into the very heart of God's reality for us. When Jesus speaks these foundational words, He unveils a beautiful truth: the only way to genuinely connect with our loving Father is through Him, the very essence of divine truth is found in Him, and the vibrant, eternal life we are so generously offered flows directly from Him. He is our welcoming entrance, the clear path into God's presence, our ultimate and unwavering truth that guides us through every season, and the unending wellspring from which all true life originates. Every breath we take, every step of our faith, and every joyful connection we experience with God is wonderfully made possible through Christ.

For God, with boundless love and divine intention, has centered all things—all His purposes, all His promises, and all His gifts—upon His beloved Son, Christ Jesus. What God so graciously bestows upon us *is* Christ Himself. In this glorious reality, truly, nothing else holds the same ultimate significance or transformative power. Yet, so often in the rich and unfolding journey of our faith, we can inadvertently find ourselves becoming preoccupied with the "small stuff": perhaps the fleeting trends of the day, the popular "buzzwords" that fade with time, or even the comfortable rhythms of rituals that, while perhaps comforting, don't draw us into deeper intimacy with God. These things, though not inherently bad, can sometimes distract us from the core, living essence of our faith, potentially keeping us from the profound closeness with God our hearts truly yearn for.

"I am the Way, and the Truth, and the Life; no one comes to the Father except through Me" (John 14:6).
This isn't merely a statement, but a loving invitation into the very heart of God's reality for us.

This is why it's a powerful and freeing invitation to pray for God to graciously help us truly, deeply *see* His Son – to perceive Him not just with our minds, but with a spiritual understanding that transforms our hearts. At its purest, most profound, and most empowering level, the Christian life is knowing Jesus, and continues to know Him deeper. It's not primarily about how many spiritual techniques we master, how perfectly we memorize theological doctrines, or even how many astounding miracles we witness or participate in. While these elements can certainly be part of our experience, the vibrant, beating heart of it all is a living, growing, personal knowledge of God's Son. When we truly begin to know Jesus – *He* who *is* the way, *He* who *is* the truth, *He* who *is* the life – our strength, our peace, and our capacity to live victoriously flows naturally from that precious, dynamic relationship. God's ultimate gift to us isn't a collection of disparate things, or temporary blessings that can be counted; it is His very own Son, given without reserve for our complete flourishing. The glorious bottom line, the central and most liberating truth of our spiritual lives, is simply and beautifully "knowing Jesus". This knowledge is not just intellectual; it is deeply experiential and profoundly life changing.

God's Way: A Living Relationship, Not a Static Formula

This profound truth—that Jesus *is* the way, our beautiful and divinely appointed "method"— undergirds and illuminates our entire relationship with God. It's crucial for our hearts to deeply embrace that this isn't about adhering to a rigid formula, a list of dos and don'ts, or following a strict set of external rules. Rather, it is about embracing a *Person*, a living, vibrant, and continuously unfolding connection with the Lord Jesus Christ Himself. This personal relationship, wonderfully established and nurtured through heartfelt faith in Jesus, isn't a singular, static event that happens once and then is set aside. Instead, it blossoms into a dynamic, continuous journey of discovering and knowing Him more intimately and deeply each day. Therefore, a consistent and joyful growth in this living knowledge of Christ is not just beneficial, but absolutely essential for cultivating a deeper, more profound relationship with our heavenly Father; it is the ongoing, exciting, and truly transformative path of discipleship.

Sometimes, in our earnestness and desire for spiritual progress, we might be tempted to seek spiritual "hacks" or quick fixes, hoping to bypass the process of deep relationship. We might hear inspiring stories or powerful sermons and look for the secret recipe. For example, after a powerful message about finding victory through Christ rather than through our own strenuous self-effort, one sincerely could say "I've felt defeated for years, but today, I finally discovered a way to victory! Thank God, now I know how! It's through the Lord, not me!". It is true, but if the truth of victory through Christ is applied in our own ways (our mindsets and strengths), then it is just a method, and we will experience defeat again. The truth that we have victory in Christ must be experienced through God's way, which is Christ himself — *we have victory in Christ and through Christ.*

We are often captivated and genuinely inspired by the stories of others—their transformative experiences of faith, their victories, and their testimonies of God's faithfulness. Yet, sometimes, in our admiration, we might inadvertently miss the most vital element—the genuine, profound, and often unseen spiritual connection with Jesus that truly fueled their journey and brought forth their fruit. When we miss this crucial understanding, we might find ourselves feeling stuck, discouraged, or not making the spiritual progress we so deeply long for. The liberating truth, the core principle we need to grasp with both our minds and our hearts, is this: *it's not ultimately about the how*—the steps, the processes, the external techniques, or the formulas—*but profoundly about the who*—the very Person of Jesus Christ. The pivotal question becomes:

with whom do we cultivate a deep, living, and dynamic spiritual connection? It must be, without reservation or substitute, with the Lord Jesus Himself. In essence, are we truly walking *in* "the way" that *is* Christ?

Consider the vital distinction between simply believing *about* Jesus (an intellectual assent) and truly believing *in* Jesus (a relational trust), a living faith that radically transforms. One person might truly *get* it – they humbly and honestly see themselves, perhaps recognizing areas where they have fallen short, felt lost, or experienced brokenness. In that moment of genuine awareness and profound humility, they surrender their need, their brokenness, and their deepest longings, wholeheartedly trusting Jesus to do what seems utterly impossible within them. And in that beautiful, courageous act of surrender, they discover an incredible, unshakeable peace with God, a peace that transcends understanding. It's a truly life-changing experience, a profound shift from anxious striving to joyful resting in His grace.

The core principle we need to grasp with both our minds and our hearts, is this: it's not ultimately about the how—the steps, the processes, the external techniques, or the formulas—but profoundly about the who—the very Person of Jesus Christ.

Then, another sincere person might hear this powerful story, genuinely longing for that same peace and freedom. They might pray earnestly for God to reveal their own shortcomings and diligently try to believe and follow what they've heard. But, to their confusion, nothing seems to happen or change in a lasting way. Why? Because the first person experienced *real* faith, a living, active, and intensely personal connection with Jesus. The second person, while undeniably sincere in their desire, might have inadvertently focused on meticulously replicating a formula or a method they heard about. They didn't *actually*, in their heart of hearts, connect with the living Person of Jesus. They may have intellectually grasped the steps, but missed the vibrant, internal heart of the matter. A method, however well-intentioned or perfectly executed, without the indwelling presence of Christ, is like a beautifully crafted but empty vessel; it's not Jesus, and it simply cannot bring about true, lasting spiritual change or profound satisfaction.

It's a liberating truth to understand that anything spiritual that is not profoundly rooted in and flowing from Christ is, in essence, like a beautiful but ultimately lifeless thing. Let us deeply underscore this vital point. Sometimes, sincere people might quietly wonder within their hearts: "How strange it is that another person believes God and their prayer is answered, while I too believe and pray, yet often feel unheard or unseen? Why does God seem so gracious to them and not to me?" It might feel, at times, as though God is showing partiality, yet the deeper, more compassionate truth is that what we might be unknowingly relying on could be merely a "thing" – perhaps a specific spiritual technique, a particular approach to prayer, or a borrowed formula from someone else's experience – and therefore, it inherently lacks true spiritual life. Neither formulas nor external methods, no matter how clever or appealing, can truly work in the dynamic spiritual realm; only Christ is living, vibrant, and eternally life-giving. Even if one has meticulously learned a whole set of spiritual techniques or theological doctrines, they are not thereby "educated" to be a Christian, because God's beloved children are *born* of the Spirit through faith in Christ, not simply taught or trained into a religious way of life.

"I am the way," so powerfully asserts the Lord Jesus.

Christ *is* our way, and Christ *is* our true, living God's method. Dear friends, let us honestly ask ourselves: Is Christ truly *my* way, the very path I walk daily, and is He truly *my* method, the source and means of all I do? Or am I, at times, leaning on a "way" or a "method" that is separate from His living presence? We can rejoice and give profound thanks that if Christ is genuinely our God's method, then everything we undertake will be imbued with His spiritual success and bring forth abundant, lasting fruit. But if what we rely on is just a method – however good, accurate, and seemingly incomparable it may be – if it is not rooted in and flowing from the living Christ, it still remains spiritually inert and has no lasting spiritual value. The reason for many prayers that seem unanswered and testimonies that feel ineffective is often found in our not truly *touching* the Lord Himself. We may have sincerely copied the methods or practices of others, hoping for their results, but we might not have yet deeply connected with the Lord Himself.

Another example: Someone that genuinely knows the Lord was sharing a profound message on Romans in a certain gathering. After hearing the message, one person excitedly shared, "Today, I finally understand the way to victory! I have a new clarity now. I believe from now on, I won't be defeated like I was before." This person had received a method, a clear understanding. Another person came to the preacher and nodded his head a little, a quiet contemplation in his eyes. When he was asked how he felt, he replied, "I do not know how to describe it. But the Lord has opened my eyes. Though I cannot say I have seen Him with perfect clarity, I dare not say I have not seen Him either." What this second brother obtained was not merely a method, a set of instructions, but a genuine, internal encounter with the Lord Himself. Consequently, he firmly maintained his spiritual ground and experienced lasting transformation, while the first person, who had only received a method and not the

Lord Himself, unfortunately may struggle again; for the method alone, without the living Christ, had no enduring value. Consider the words of Jesus in Luke 18:9-14 — The Pharisee stood by himself and prayed: 'God, I thank you that I am not like other people—robbers, evildoers, adulterers—or even like this tax collector.' ...But the tax collector stood at a distance. He would not even look up to heaven, but beat his breast and said, 'God, have mercy on me, a sinner.'

Is Christ truly my way, the very path I walk daily, and is He truly my method, the source and means of all I do? Or am I, at times, leaning on a "way" or a "method" that is separate from His living presence?

Many times, even the sincere motive behind our hearing a message can be subtly erroneous. Instead of humbly asking the Lord for a divine revelation that we may truly *see* Him, we might primarily try with our intellect to memorize a method or a teaching to take back with us, hoping it will bring us spiritual success. And even if we diligently follow that method, we may find ourselves getting nowhere in terms of true, inward spiritual life. Sometimes, though, we do seem to catch a glimpse, a moment of insight, perhaps without having any great assurance to dare to say definitively that we have *seen* the Lord. Nevertheless, in those precious moments, we *do* see Him, and such genuine, inward insight brings about real, lasting change in our hearts and lives. Thank the Lord, this is the true way — not that we have merely learned a method or a set of instructions, but that we have come to truly *know* the Lord Himself. It is clearly and beautifully shown to us in His Word and through the witness of the Spirit that the Lord Himself *is* the method, the means, and the end of our spiritual journey.

For this profound reason, then, we should, upon hearing a message, a testimony, or even engaging with the Scriptures, gently and honestly examine ourselves. The crucial question is: have we truly encountered the Lord Himself in a living way, or have we merely understood a method, a concept, or a teaching? There is no true, lasting deliverance, no genuine freedom, in merely knowing a method, no matter how accurate or well-presented it is. True deliverance, profound peace, and lasting transformation are found only in knowing the Lord. Listening to how He has helped others, while often inspiring, will not save us; it is our personal, heartfelt trusting in the Lord alone that is truly effectual and brings salvation. The words describing a method and the words describing knowing the Lord may sometimes sound about the same on the surface, yet their actualities, their inward realities, are worlds apart. The Lord is the Lord of life, the source and sustainer of all true existence, especially spiritual life. Whoever truly touches Him, touches life – vibrant, eternal, and abundant life. Touching the Lord alone, in genuine faith and surrender, is what truly gives life to our souls.

Christ Is the Truth: Our Liberating Reality and Foundation

The Lord Jesus, in His magnificent self-revelation, not only introduces Himself as the way, our divine path to God, but He also profoundly speaks of Himself as the truth. This "truth" is far more expansive and dynamic than a mere collection of facts, doctrines, or theological statements *about* Christ. No, the glorious reality is that it is Christ Himself who *is* the truth, the living embodiment of all that is real, authentic, and divine. How often, in our genuine pursuit of understanding, do we as Christians inadvertently take the teaching and the interpretations of Christ as the ultimate truths, when in actuality, truth is not simply the relating of a concept or a thing, but is the very Person of Christ Himself?

"And you will know the [divine] **Truth, and the Truth will set you free,"** says the Lord (John 8:32). Let us gently and honestly consider: how many abstract truths or intellectual understandings have actually made us truly, deeply free in our inner being? The infallible Word of God states with absolute certainty that the truth shall make us free, yet how many times does "truth" remain merely a doctrine to us, a concept we grasp with our minds, but which doesn't translate into a liberating experience? Our spiritual eyes may not yet have been fully opened to truly *see* Christ as the living Truth. We may have talked about many profound doctrines for years, perhaps even a decade or more, yet we may still not have genuinely seen Him in that truth. We may have diligently listened to profound teachings for an equal length of time, and yet again, we might not have had that transformative encounter. People may be able to articulately speak on the doctrine of co-death with Christ, discussing its theological intricacies, without truly knowing the profound, delivering power of this death in their own lives. Or they may converse eloquently on resurrection life without personally experiencing its vibrant, dynamic power at work within them. If all we engage with and talk about is doctrine detached from the living Christ, then, in essence, we are handling something that remains intellectually stimulating but spiritually inert, something that is, in a spiritual sense, dead.

Let's consider a practical illustration. Imagine once a person wrote you a message seeking spiritual counsel, as follows: "My friend has sinned against me, and I am not clear whether I should forgive him. I therefore ask you to instruct me. My heart is quite composed before God. If you say I should forgive, I will forgive him. If you think I should not, then I will not forgive him." Brethren, what is your genuine opinion about such a Christian's approach? Is it a living response? Consider another hypothetical scenario: Suppose the one dearest to me is gone, and so I write a message to another person inquiring thus: "He who is dearest to me is dead; should I therefore mourn? If you say I should cry, I will cry; but if you say no, then I will not cry." Most certainly you, with your natural human compassion, would gently smile or even laugh at such an inquiry, for it is deeply absurd. If a person cries or does not cry solely according to what they are told to do, then neither their mourning nor their lack of mourning is real. Both are false, devoid of genuine emotion, and are therefore merely dead works, not an outflow of authentic life. In our relationship with a person, you either forgive from a heart moved by Christ, or you do not. Whenever we act solely on a dead doctrine, without the living truth of Christ transforming us from within, it becomes a mere pretense, a performance lacking spiritual vitality.

Dear friends, let us grasp this profound and liberating principle: whatever is not Christ living in us, or is not Christ Himself as our truth—that is to say, whatever is done solely on the basis of a doctrine, a rule, or an external understanding—is, in the spiritual realm, dead work. It has no true life flowing through it; it is not authentically living. Do you perceive the critical difference here? It is a difference too vast, too significant, to go unnoticed in our spiritual walk. External "work" often requires our memory, our conscious effort to recall and apply a principle; but genuine, spiritual *life* acts spontaneously, from an inner wellspring. A word spoken out of true spiritual life is not propelled by our memory trying to recite a doctrine; rather, it is motivated by a divine power and a living Person within us. The Lord Himself, not merely doctrine or teaching, is meant to be in active control over us, guiding our every thought, word, and deed. There *must* be a day when God, in His grace, opens our spiritual eyes to truly perceive that all spiritual reality, all authentic power, all liberating truth, is found *in Christ* alone. We are not called to constantly try to remember certain doctrines and strive to act accordingly; instead, it is Christ who lives in us, and He is our truth. Therefore, when He acts through us, it is living, spontaneous, and genuinely transformative.

Whatever is done solely on the basis of a doctrine, a rule,
or an external understanding is, in the spiritual realm,
dead work.

Consider a person who was deeply offended by another person. He could not abide the offense, and so he heatedly scolded the offender in a moment of frustration. Afterwards, as is often the case, his conscience was ill at ease; he felt a sincere conviction that he should go to the offender and apologize. But as he recalled the details of how that person had so deeply offended him, his anger was again stirred, and his resolve wavered. Meanwhile, the inner burden remained; he still felt he truly owed the other person an apology, yet the anger made a face-to-face meeting difficult. So he decided to write a message to him, believing this was the right, Christian thing to do. He got his phone and began to write: "I feel it is wrong for me to have scolded you." But even as he wrote, as he was reminded once more of how truly wrong that person was who had so deeply offended him, his anger once more returned, simmering beneath the surface. After waiting a while, trying to compose himself, he took up his phone and continued to write, completing the apology. Yet, during the entire time of writing he still was annoyed, a deep-seated resentment still lingering in his heart. By all outward appearances, this message looked like one beautifully written by a Christian, expressing regret, though we who understand spiritual realities know it was the result of a *doctrine* being applied, not of true, spontaneous spiritual life flowing. Although he wrote an apology, his heart remained filled with wrath and unresolved bitterness. Should he meet that person, he might offer a polite greeting and shake hands, yet inwardly the controversy had not truly passed away, and so his words and demeanor could not possibly be natural, free, or genuinely warm. Do we now clearly see the difference? The Lord *is* the truth. If ever it be merely doctrine or an intellectual concept, and not the living Lord Himself, it is spiritually dead. May we realize this profound distinction: in all spiritual matters, *with* the Lord it is life, but *without* the Lord it is death. If a thing is done as a beautiful result of His grace shining and active working in us, then this thing is genuinely living, bearing the fruit of His eternal life.

Christ Is the Life: Our Abundant, Effortless Wellspring

Following the words "I am the way and the truth," the Lord continues with the equally vital declaration, "and the life." As we meditate on this, we are gently reminded of a fundamental spiritual truth: true, divine life issues forth spontaneously and effortlessly into beautiful works, but our human "work" can never, ever be a substitute for life itself. We ought to be crystal clear on this foundational point: our striving or our actions are not life—for life is inherently effortless, a natural outflow when Christ Himself is truly living within us. How often we, as sincere Christians, can find ourselves toiling and striving to embody spiritual virtues! How we can become weary and burdened through our daily exertion to "be" a Christian. It can feel as though certain doctrines or expectations are most severe, for they seem to demand of us to somehow generate humility, cultivate patience, force ourselves to be forgiving, and extend long-suffering through our own willpower. These demands can literally wear us out, leaving us feeling exhausted and inadequate. Many sincere believers might concede that to be a Christian is a difficult task, fraught with struggle. This is especially true for young believers, full of zeal but perhaps lacking understanding of this deeper truth. The more they try in their own strength, the more difficult and frustrating it can become. And after having tried for a length of time, they may still bear no true resemblance to the vibrant, joyful Christian they long to be. Dear reader, if Christ is not genuinely our life, then indeed, we will feel compelled to do all the spiritual "work" in our own strength; but if He *is* life, then we do not need to struggle in that way, for His life flows naturally. Again, let us affirm this liberating truth: life is Christ Himself, and our human work can never substitute for His divine life.

There is a grave and often pervasive mistake among God's beloved children. Many mistakenly regard "life" as something which they must diligently do, achieve, or perform in their own strength, believing that without their striving, there will be no spiritual life evident. Yet, what all of us should truly realize is that if there is the living, vibrant presence of Christ as life within us, there will not be the slightest need for our own strenuous "doing," but rather, that divine life will naturally and beautifully flow forth. Consider for a moment the effortless wonder of how our physical eyes see and our ears hear. Our eyes see most naturally, and our ears hear spontaneously, not because we "try" to make them do so, but simply because there is life within them. We must be crystal clear on this profound point: true, spiritual life naturally flows into beautiful works and virtues, but our works are never, ever a substitute for His life. In fact, sometimes our "work" in spiritual matters might inadvertently prove the *absence* of true spiritual life or reveal its weakness.

Life will genuinely issue in good morals and righteous conduct, but good morals, however commendable, are no stand-in for the source of life itself—Christ. For example, a person may be outwardly very gentle, moderate, and reserved in his demeanor. Someone might praise him, saying, "This person's life is not bad, it's quite commendable." But this praise, while well-intentioned, might use the wrong terminology. For the Lord says, "I am the life." However gentle, moderate, and reserved this person may be in his natural disposition, if these qualities do not genuinely flow from Christ Himself living within him or her, they are not truly reckoned as spiritual life in God's eyes. It is perfectly true to say this person has a good temper, or rarely causes any trouble, or always treats people kindly and never quarrels; but it cannot be said of him or her, on the basis of these natural traits alone, that he or she has a rich spiritual life. If these good things are merely natural, products of his or her upbringing, personality, or self-discipline, they are not Christ as life, for they do not come from the divine source of Christ.

If Christ is not genuinely our life, then indeed, we will feel compelled to do all the spiritual "work" in our own strength; but if He is life, then we do not need to struggle in that way, for His life flows naturally.

Other people cherish another thought, a different conclusion about life. They surmise that spiritual life is simply power. To have the Lord as our life, they believe, means to be given power by Him to *do* good things. Nevertheless, God's Word beautifully shows us that our spiritual power is not merely a "thing" or an ability that we possess; it is simply Christ Himself. Our power is not an abstract strength to accomplish tasks; rather, it *is* a living Person. Life to us is not only power in a general sense but also profoundly a Person. It is Christ who manifests Himself in us, working through us, instead of using Christ as a means to display our own good works or accomplishments.

Hopefully we may clearly see that true spiritual life is neither mere emotional excitement nor merely profound, thoughtful words. Words of wisdom, clever sayings, logical arguments, and thoughtful dissertations, while valuable, are not necessarily life in and of themselves. So it is not a surprise that some will inquire, "How strange that life is neither fervor nor elevating thought. Where, then, can we find life? What is life after all?" We confess we do not have a better, more complete way to express this profound matter of holding forth life than to say it is Christ Himself. All we can truly say is that it is something infinitely deeper than fleeting emotion and far more profound than intellectual thought. And once one genuinely meets this "something," he will instantly be quickened within, a deep inner knowing and vitality will awaken. This "something" is called life, and it is a Person: Jesus Christ.

So, what truly *is* life? Life is more profound than thought; our intellect can never fully grasp or surpass life's divine essence. It also is deeper than emotion; our feelings, however strong, are superficial in comparison with the depth of true life. Whether we are speaking of thought or emotion, they are relatively external and temporary aspects of our being. What, then, is life? The Lord Jesus definitively declared: "I am the life." We should be cautious not to hastily conclude that we have truly met life when all we meet is a kind of "atmosphere," such as a so-called spiritually or emotionally charged atmosphere in a gathering. Only Christ *is* life; the rest, in comparison to Him, is not.

Therefore, we need to diligently learn the vital lesson of truly knowing life in its purest form. For life depends not on how enthusiastic our emotions are, or on how manifold and extensive our thoughts are; it rests exclusively on whether the Lord has genuinely manifested His own self within us. There is therefore nothing more important, nothing more central to our spiritual journey, than to truly know the Lord. As we are deeply knowing Him, we are intimately touching life itself. We ought to see before God the profound and beautiful meaning of Christ being our life. Those who are easily excitable or especially clever are not necessarily the people who deeply know the Lord. Knowing Him requires a spiritual seeing, an inward revelation by the Holy Spirit. Such seeing *is* life, and it miraculously transforms us from within. If we truly know the Lord as our life, we realize the utter futility, the beautiful uselessness, of all our natural efforts in spiritual matters. Hence, we learn to lovingly and joyfully look to Him alone, relying entirely on His indwelling life.

When we first believed in the Lord, we often did not fully realize what truly "looking to Him" meant in practice. But gradually, as we grow in grace and understanding, we learn increasingly to look to Him, having recognized with growing conviction that everything—every spiritual virtue, every victory, every moment of genuine growth, every aspect of our spiritual reality— depends entirely upon Christ, and not upon our own strength or efforts. In the beginning of our Christian walk, it was natural to desire to possess one spiritual "thing" after another; we often found it challenging to trust Him for *everything*. After we learned a bit more through experience and the gentle teaching of the Spirit, however, we received some deeper understanding as to the profound necessity of trusting Him. This trust is not primarily in the sense of believing Him to grant us item after item from a spiritual wish list, but rather, it is in the far more liberating sense of trusting Him to *do* what we are utterly unable to do by ourselves. When we first became a Christian, we were often inclined to do everything ourselves, driven by a subtle fear lest nothing would ever be truly done, or that matters would somehow fall to pieces if we did not personally take charge and exert our will. Hence, we were often working, striving, and toiling all the time in our own strength. Later, in having had our spiritual eyes opened to truly *see* the Lord to be our life, we come to a place of deep inner knowing that all authentic spiritual reality is *of Christ* and not *of us*. Consequently, we learn to truly rest in Him and to lovingly, joyfully look to Him alone as the source and sustainer of all.

What truly is life? Life is more profound than thought; our intellect can never fully grasp or surpass life's divine essence. It also is deeper than emotion; our feelings, however strong, are superficial in comparison with the depth of true life.

Let us keep in the forefront of our hearts and minds this glorious truth: instead of giving us one object after another, God, in His infinite wisdom and boundless love, gives His Son to us. Because of this magnificent reality, we can always lift up our hearts and look to the Lord with genuine faith and tender affection, saying from the depths of our being, "Lord, you are my way; Lord, you are my truth; Lord, you are my life. It is *you*, Lord, who is intimately related to me, not your things." May we constantly ask God to give us the grace, the inward enabling, that we may truly *see* Christ in all spiritual things, in every aspect of our walk. Day by day, as we grow in this seeing, we become increasingly convinced, with a settled peace, that aside from Christ there is no true way, nor truth, nor life. How easily, in our human frailty, we can make things—external practices, doctrines, feelings—as our way, truth, and life. Or, we might call a "certain atmosphere" or a surge of emotion as life; we might label clear, logical thought as life. We might consider strong emotion or outward conduct as life. In reality, though, these are not life in their purest, divine form. We ought to realize, with a profound sense of liberation, that *only* the Lord is life. Christ is our life, our very spiritual existence. And it is the Lord Himself who lives out this life in us.

"I have been crucified with Christ and I no longer live, but Christ lives in me. The life I now live in the body, I live by faith in the Son of God, who loved me and gave himself for me" (Galatians 2:20 NIV).

Dear Father, I humble myself before you and confess that I have sinned by seeking a **way**, a **method**, or a **formula** apart from your Son, Jesus Christ.

I repent of my striving to acquire spiritual "things" and virtues through my own efforts, religious duties, and external techniques. I confess that I have often relied on a spiritual "fix", looking to my own strength or the life of others instead of the living Person of Christ. I truly regret treating your grace as merely a supply to replenish my lacks, rather than embracing Christ as your *total* and *only* Gift, the sole provision for my entire life.

I turn away from the empty vessels of my own methods and, in true repentance, I wholeheartedly receive your Son. I surrender my reliance on anything separate from Him, for I believe the liberating truth that **He is the Way, the Truth, and the Life**. I receive Him now as my Way, the living path to you; my Truth, the reality that sets me free; and my Life, the constant, effortless source of all I need. Thank you for making my journey a restful, intimate relationship with the Person of Jesus, my All in All.

In His mighty name, I pray. Amen.

4

Resurrection Life

In a deeply comforting and profoundly powerful exchange with Martha, Jesus declared, **"I am the Resurrection and the Life; whoever believes in** (adheres to, trusts in, relies on) **Me, although he may die, yet he will live"** (John 11:25, AMP).

John Chapter 11 beautifully reveals how the Lord Jesus gave life to one who was already dead—in other words, how He raised Lazarus from the grave. He certainly possessed the unfathomable ability to raise the dead and He indeed caused a dead man to be resurrected. Yet, instead of emphasizing His *power* by saying, "I can raise the dead," He profoundly stated, **"I am the Resurrection."** Shortly after this glorious declaration, He powerfully demonstrated this truth by indeed raising Lazarus from the dead. Both Martha and Mary, grieving sisters, were present on that monumental day. From their human perspective, steeped in sorrow and longing, it might have seemed far more appropriate and comforting for the Lord Jesus to simply say, "Do not worry about your brother's death, for I can and will raise him up." We, too, often find ourselves longing to hear such words – a promise of what God *will do* for us. What we often admire and eagerly anticipate is that God will perform extraordinary acts on our behalf. Frequently, our heartfelt prayers and expectations before God are focused on the promise that the Lord will do through and so for us, addressing our specific needs and situations. Yet, the Lord especially wishes for us to deeply *see* and grasp that it is not primarily about what He *can do*, but rather about what He Himself *is*, for His doing, His powerful actions, are always fundamentally rooted in and flow directly from His glorious being.

Consider the poignant example of Martha. She possessed a commendable belief in the Lord's power. She earnestly said to Him, "**Lord, if You had been here, my brother would not have died**" (John 11:21, AMP). And Mary, too, shared a similar belief in His power (John 11:32). But in their human understanding, both sisters, though sincere, initially failed to fully perceive that the Lord Himself *is* the Resurrection and the Life. May we, with opened hearts, grasp this liberating truth: all that God can possibly do, every miracle, every provision, every act of restoration, is intrinsically included in *who He is*. People often do not receive the full, dynamic power of God because they do not yet fully know *who He is* in His glorious Person. As the Scripture beautifully reminds us, "But without faith it is impossible to please and be satisfactory to Him, for whoever would come to God \[must believe\] that He exists and that He is the rewarder of those who diligently seek Him" (Hebrews 11:6, AMP).

The Lord especially wishes for us to deeply see and grasp that it is not primarily about what He can do, but rather about what He Himself is.

What the Lord Jesus wishes to tell us here is not merely that He is *able* to preserve one's life, but that He Himself *is* life; not just that He *can* raise the dead, but that He Himself *is* resurrection. Let us, with humble and earnest hearts, ask God to open our spiritual eyes to truly see *who the Lord is*. It is absolutely imperative for us to see, before the very presence of God, that Christ is truly *everything* to us. With such a profound and transformative understanding, we will make real, lasting progress in all spiritual matters. It is absolutely essential for us to realize that with God, there is no "thing" apart from Christ, no separate blessing or power that exists independently of Him! Our genuine progress in spiritual matters deeply depends on our truly grasping this spiritual reality—do we know God Himself, or do we primarily know only the things which God has done, or what He can do?

The central and most profound theme of John Chapter 11 is not merely a historical account of *how* the Lord Jesus raised up Lazarus, but rather a profound revelation of *how He Himself was resurrection to Lazarus*. Do we see the crucial distinction here? The Lord *is* the resurrection. Because He *was* resurrection to Lazarus, Lazarus was, therefore, resurrected. He had not merely given something called "resurrection" to Lazarus as an external gift; He *was* Himself the very essence and power of resurrection to Lazarus. In other words, what the Lord *did* was the external manifestation, but what He Himself *was* the divine substance, the living reality behind the action. We are not suggesting that the Lord Jesus did not physically raise Lazarus from the dead; we simply maintain that He *was* resurrection to him, and that *therefore* Lazarus was raised from the dead.

It is vitally important for us to understand that all of God's magnificent workings in and through Christ are profoundly embodied in this singular, glorious principle. Because the Lord *is* that "thing" (that virtue, that power, that life) in us, therefore we *have* that thing. It is a divine order: First, the *being* (Christ Himself dwelling in us), and then, the *having* (the spontaneous outflow of His nature through us). Many Christians, with good intentions, tend to talk about the Giver and His gifts as separate entities. But one day, in a glorious moment of spiritual revelation, we find out that the Giver is Himself His gift, the ultimate and most precious gift. For God does not bring out many and various items to give to us in fragmented pieces; what He generously and completely gives is Christ Himself. It is truly a blessed day if and when our spiritual eyes are opened to fully recognize this profound truth—that *all* things, all spiritual realities, all divine virtues, are profoundly *in Christ*.

John 11 is not merely a historical account of how the Lord Jesus raised up Lazarus, but rather a profound revelation of how He Himself was resurrection to Lazarus.

Here the Lord powerfully declares *who He is*. He says, **"I am the Resurrection and the Life"** (John 11:25, AMP). Since He *is* the Resurrection, it presents no problem whatever for Lazarus to be raised up, for the source of resurrection is intrinsically present in Him. We wholeheartedly believe the Lord did indeed raise Lazarus from the dead, but the profound emphasis was on *having the Lord Himself* as that Resurrection. The physical resurrection of Lazarus is truly a wonderful phenomenon, a testimony that it can and will be done again; but knowing the Lord Jesus as Resurrection, as the very essence of overcoming death, is a matter of infinitely greater and eternal significance. Many people can intellectually believe the Lord Jesus as a life-giver, one who *gives* life, but to truly believe Him *as life* itself is quite another matter, a deeper, more transformative reality. He not only is the life-giver, He also *is* life itself. He is the very life He gives, as well as the Giver of life. He is both the Lord *of* resurrection and the resurrection *itself*. As soon as we truly touch this liberating truth, we instantly comprehend with an inner knowing that whatever is in Christ is living, vibrant, and eternally real. What God universally gives to humankind is Christ Himself. We earnestly hope and pray that we may have at least a glorious ray of light flash in upon our hearts, causing us to realize, in the depths of our being, that the Lord truly *is* all. "**I am the Resurrection and the Life**," declares our Lord. These two magnificent realities—Resurrection and Life—encompass and include the entire Bible; therefore, knowing Resurrection and Life in Christ is truly a matter of great spiritual importance and eternal consequence.

Christ Is Life: The Essence of Our Being

In the breathtaking garden of Eden, God, in His perfect design, placed the man He had lovingly created. Before this man lay two profound possibilities, representing the ultimate choice: he might experience divine life, or he might choose death. If he ate the fruit of the tree of the knowledge of good and evil, he was warned that he would surely die; but if he ate the fruit of the tree of life, he would possess and experience life in its truest, fullest sense. The man whom God created was indeed good, perfectly formed and innocent, but there yet remained a deciding, pivotal issue—that of life and death, of partaking of God's own divine life or remaining in his natural, though good, existence. At that momentous time, he was perfectly capable of thinking, reasoning, and physical movement, but, fundamentally, he did not yet have *life* in the spiritual sense represented by the tree of life. We do not mean to say that he was not alive naturally, for judging by man's natural, physical life, he certainly was living. Genesis 2:7 (AMP) clearly tells us that "**the Lord God formed man from the dust of the ground, and breathed into his nostrils the breath of life; and man became a living being** \[an individual, with a soul, functioning as a living personality\]." Nonetheless, judging by what is profoundly represented and symbolized in the tree of life, he had not yet received *divine life* as a spiritual reality within him. He possessed the power of thinking and feeling—these constituting the main, vibrant functions of man's soul—yet he did not possess the *life* as eternally symbolized by the tree of life. Here, through this ancient, foundational narrative, we are profoundly instructed that divine life is infinitely deeper than mere emotion and far more profound and expansive than human thought.

Everything precious and authentic in Christianity seems to have its counterfeit—a shadow imitating the substance. We see false repentance, hollow confessions, superficial conversions, fleeting zeal, self-serving love, even deceptive works of the Holy Spirit, imitation gifts of the Holy Spirit, and tragically, even counterfeit life. How many sincere Christians, in their earnestness, might inadvertently regard good feeling or strong emotional sensations as the very essence of life! They might mistakenly esteem a "certain atmosphere" in a gathering or a loud, fervent voice as being inherently full of spiritual life. They struggle to distinguish between true divine life and mere feeling, not recognizing that the former is infinitely much deeper, more foundational, and more enduring than the latter. Another sincere class of Christians will reckon noble, insightful thought, or perhaps even strong, moving emotion, as life. If they find in a message many provocative thoughts, intellectually interesting words, and commendable, logical arguments, they might deem it to be the presence of true life. But those who are truly experienced in the ways of God and who have genuinely learned through the Spirit will, with loving wisdom, inform us that true life is profoundly deeper than transient feeling or intellectual thought alone. Moreover, life is not merely action or activity. Not because one is extremely lively, outwardly enthusiastic, and perpetually active in ministry can he necessarily be termed to be genuinely "in life." The person may indeed be engaging in much action, but this external activity, if devoid of the inward source, cannot be labeled true divine life. Man in this instance is working, striving, and performing instead of simply living out the spontaneous, effortless outflow of Christ's life within him.

Life is therefore not any matter outside of Christ; it is Christ Himself. If it is merely a thing, an abstract concept, or an external practice, it is, in a spiritual sense, dead.

Now, we do not, by any means, insinuate here that there is no thought, no feeling, and no action in a life lived in Christ; we simply would affirm with unwavering conviction that true divine life is *neither* merely feeling, *nor* merely thought, *nor* merely action. You may hear the same good, scriptural word, yet in one person you sense the vibrant presence of life flowing through their articulation, while in the other, you perceive only intellectual thought, however clear and precise. You may witness a stirred, emotional response in one person, yet meet true, profound life in another. Many sincere brethren deem certain sensations within them as true life, but those who have genuinely learned from the Spirit know better that this is just not so; feelings are good but fleeting and can be deceptive. Many also regard certain profound thoughts within them to be life, but experienced believers, having tasted the depth of Christ, will lovingly pronounce this as not true divine life at all.

There are so many who, in their sincerity, think that since they say similar words or hold similar beliefs, they are bound to be the same in spiritual reality. But this is not true. It is entirely possible for the same words to be mere thought in one person, yet truly life in another, flowing from Christ Himself. **"I am the Life**,**"** says the Lord (John 14:6, AMP). Life is therefore not any matter *outside* of Christ; it is Christ Himself. If it is merely a thing, an abstract concept, or an external practice, it is, in a spiritual sense, dead. The "life" which many Christians talk about and strive for is often but a thing they themselves produce through their own efforts or natural abilities, not the spontaneous outflow of His divine presence.

How we truly, desperately need the tender mercy of the Lord in this crucial respect. We know what thought is, what feeling is, and what activity is; yet, so often, we lack a clear, experiential appreciation of what divine life truly is in its essence. May we, with humble and longing hearts, ask the Lord to graciously show us what life really is—to grant us a revelation of Christ as our life. And one glorious day, when we are given such a profound, inward revelation by His Spirit, we will naturally and instinctively know what life is, no longer needing definitions or explanations, and then, in that knowing, we are truly able to touch the Lord Himself as our living reality.

As for you, the anointing [the special gift, the preparation] which you received from Him remains [permanently] in you, and you have no need for anyone to teach you. But just as His anointing teaches you [giving you insight through the presence of the Holy Spirit] about all things, and is true and is not a lie, and just as His anointing has taught you, you must remain in Him [being rooted in Him, knit to Him]. (1 John 2:27 AMP)

Christ Is the Resurrection: Triumph Over Death

Let us turn our hearts and minds once more to the glorious truth of the resurrection. That which has encountered the extinguishing power of death and yet miraculously survives is called resurrection. Whatever outlives death, whatever emerges victorious from the grave, is resurrection. Death, that unwelcome intruder, came to humankind after the first man, Adam, ate the forbidden fruit from the tree of the knowledge of good and evil. Ever since that tragic moment, humanity has been utterly unable to endure death in its own strength. All who have entered the silent realm of the grave have never, by their own power, returned. Once gone, they never come back to this earthly life. In the vast expanse of the universe, among countless numbers of people who have lived and died, there has been only one, a singular and magnificent exception, who has willingly gone into death and triumphantly come out of it—and this one, this Victor over the grave, is our Lord Jesus Christ. As He Himself declared in a glorious revelation to the Apostle John, **"I am the living One; and I was dead, and behold, I am alive forevermore, and I have the keys of death and of Hades** (the underworld, the realm of the dead)" (Revelation 1:17-18, AMP).

The Lord Jesus is not merely *associated* with resurrection; He is the very Lord *of* resurrection, the source and power behind it. Resurrection speaks of a life that passes through the grim reality of death but is not, cannot be, held captive by death's power. The Bible uses the word "held" or "bound" to vividly describe the formidable power of death. People enter into death and are not able to come out again because death, like a relentless jailer, holds tightly fast all who have entered its domain. But death, in all its power, was not, and is not, able to hold Christ Jesus. Hence, His emergence from the grave is called life, a new and unconquerable kind of life, and it is also, and preeminently, called resurrection. Resurrection, in its deepest sense, is the divine life which willingly submitted to death, was laid in the tomb, and yet is alive forevermore, a perpetual and vibrant reality. Our Lord Jesus is this life, this resurrection life, precisely because He was dead—having, in His redemptive work, entered into hell, the deepest recess of the earth, the realm of the dead—yet He is alive forevermore, seated at the right hand of the Father. Death had no power to hold Him in its grip; its chains were broken, its victory undone. He comes out of death, leaving the grave empty and its power vanquished. And such a life as this, a life that has stared death in the face and emerged eternally triumphant, is called resurrection. Hence, a life which bears the undeniable marks of having passed through death and yet is gloriously and perpetually alive is the very definition of resurrection.

Quite a few sincere people, pondering the biblical accounts, are asking why it is recorded in John chapter 20 that after the Lord Jesus was raised from among the dead, He intentionally left the vivid imprint of the nails in His hands and the mark of the spear in His side for Thomas to touch and to probe. This was not a mere oversight or a lingering; it was a deliberate and powerful demonstration of the meaning of resurrection. What the Lord intended to show Thomas, and through him to all who would believe, was not simply that He had been wounded and had died, but that He had been wounded unto death and yet, behold, He is now gloriously alive, bearing in His resurrected body the very imprint of death's assault. Nonetheless, despite these marks, He is undeniably eternally alive. This, in its tangible reality, is called resurrection—life triumphing over death, bearing the scars of the battle but living in eternal victory.

Resurrection speaks of a life that passes through the grim reality of death but is not, cannot be, held captive by death's power.

Such a reality ought to be true, in a spiritual and experiential sense, in our own lives as believers who are united with Christ in His death and resurrection. We often have many things in our natural lives, our natural abilities, our self-confidence, our human strength, which do not carry the imprint of having passed through death, and therefore, they cannot, in a spiritual sense, be labeled as resurrection. Only that which bears the indelible imprint of having gone through death and yet is now alive, animated by Christ's resurrection life, is called resurrection. Do not imagine that it is truly well with you, in a spiritual sense, if you possess natural eloquence, human cleverness, and innate ability. It is quite possible for you to have all of these natural qualities—eloquence, cleverness, and ability—without the essential imprint of death having worked in them. Spiritually discerning people may judge whether or not there is genuine resurrection life at work by noting if the imprint of death, the mark of the cross, is upon our natural eloquence, our human cleverness, and our innate ability. A man may possess great natural talent and may be most capable in many areas; he may seem, in a human sense, to be very much alive and vibrant. Yet, there may be no genuine mark of death, no evidence of the cross having worked in his talent, precisely because he has such profound confidence in himself, relying on his own abilities. He trusts that he rarely, if ever, does wrong, and he is often sure of success in whatever he undertakes, leaning on his own understanding and strength. This person may possess immense self-confidence, self-reliance, self-assurance, and self-strength, but tragically, he does not yet have the essential mark of death, the brokenness that comes from encountering the cross experientially. We do not mean to say that a resurrected person, one in whom Christ's resurrection life is at work, does not have power; what we are trying to affirm here is that in the power of a risen one, there is always the undeniable sign of death having been at work. He is able to work, to minister, to serve, but he dares not, will not, rely on himself or his own strength. He can do many deeds, empowered by Christ, yet he has lost that touch of self-assurance that characterized his natural man, and his own human strength has, through the cross, been turned into a conscious weakness that makes him rely entirely on God. This, this profound transformation, we call resurrection.

In his deeply honest and humble letter to the church at Corinth, the great Apostle Paul confesses the following, revealing the mark of death and resurrection in his own life: **"And I was with you in weakness and in fear and in much trembling"** (1 Corinthians 2:3, AMP). These are not the words of a weak or insecure man in a human sense, but words spoken by one who truly knows God, who has experientially encountered the cross and the power of resurrection. How tragic it is that there are so many seemingly strong and self-confident people among believers who have not yet learned this vital lesson of weakness and reliance on Christ. But here is a man, a spiritual giant, who humbly acknowledges himself as being experientially in weakness, in fear, and in trembling before the magnitude of God's work. There is, in his very being and ministry, the undeniable mark of death having worked in his natural strength, making way for resurrection power.

Consequently, in the divine economy, resurrection and the cross are eternally inseparable. The cross, in its spiritual reality, is an eliminating power. Things which issue out of ourselves, our natural abilities, our self-reliance, our fallen nature, are utterly unable to rise again once they have gone through the cross experientially, for they are lost in death, their power broken. Only what passes through death and miraculously survives, what has the sign of death upon it and yet lives, animated by divine life, is resurrection. Resurrection, by its very nature, presupposes a passing through death, a spiritual crucifixion, and passing through death always eliminates something of the old, fallen self.

If we genuinely know, experientially, what resurrection is, we will simultaneously know the cross as a profound, eliminating power in our lives. When we pass through the cross, allowing its work to have its effect, we will be rid of many things that once characterized our natural man. We will become a totally different person, a new creation in Christ, precisely because many things, many aspects of our old self, will have been stripped away from us, left in the grave of the cross. Only that which has divine life about it, that which is born of the Spirit, may alone experience resurrection; without divine life in it, there is no possibility of resurrection. For example, in the natural realm, we may cut a block of wood into pieces and bury them in the earth. After many days, these pieces will be completely decayed and become wholly useless, returning to dust. But if we cut a living branch out of a tree and plant it in the earth, if the conditions are right, we will find it budding and growing after a while, bearing new life. One will decay and return to dust, while the other will bud forth with new life. All that is spiritually dead, that which is of the fallen human nature, will eventually be corrupted and pass away; only what is spiritually living, what is born of God and has His divine life within it, will be resurrected upon passing through death experientially with Christ. My life with Christ ought to be planted, not buried.

We may ask ourselves this question: How do I know I have died to myself? How can I know that the cross has genuinely done its work in me? The answer, though simple, is profound. If the Lord has truly worked in your life through the power of the cross, you will experientially lose many things that once defined you in your natural state. If you have remained essentially intact since you were once saved, still being as "rich" in your natural abilities and as "full" of self-confidence as before, then this plainly indicates that the cross has not yet fully worked in you, its subtracting power has not had its effect. As the cross operates in your life, you will notice what a big subtracting or cleansing work the Lord has accomplished in you, a divine stripping away of the old. And as a consequence, what you were naturally able to do before, relying on your own strength, you are now no longer able to do in the same way; what you once were supremely confident of, you presently are not so confident of in yourself, and what you originally had great natural courage in, you lately are hesitant about, not in a negative sense, but in a holy fear and reliance on God. Thus are the genuine workings of the Lord proven in a life. In case there is true resurrection in your life, then many items of your old nature, your self and its expressions, must have been left behind in the grave of the cross, since things there, things of Adam, cannot possibly survive death and emerge with new life. Whatever is of Adam, whatever is born of the flesh, cannot live upon its going into death; its end is corruption. But the divine life of the Lord Jesus is quite able to pass through death and triumphantly come out again, bringing us with Him. This, this glorious emergence bearing the marks of death overcome, is resurrection.

And when I came to you, brothers and sisters, proclaiming to you the testimony of God [concerning salvation through Christ], I did not come with superiority of speech or of wisdom [no lofty words of eloquence or of philosophy as a Greek orator might do]; for I made the decision to know nothing [that is, to forego philosophical or theological discussions regarding inconsequential things and opinions while] among you except Jesus Christ, and Him crucified [and the meaning of His redemptive, substitutionary death and His resurrection]. I came to you in [a state of] weakness and fear and great trembling. And my message and my preaching were not in persuasive words of wisdom [using clever rhetoric], but [they were delivered] in demonstration of the [Holy] Spirit [operating through me] and of [His] power [stirring the minds of the listeners and persuading them], so that your faith would not rest on the wisdom and rhetoric of men, but on the power of God. (1 Corinthians 2:1-5 AMP)

Sometimes, things that were lost in death, things of true value that were corrupted by the fall, are regained and restored in Christ through resurrection. It is like the branch which, when cut off from a tree, appears dead and lifeless, but which, when planted in the earth and nurtured, will once again grow and bud, bearing fruit. So, by our saying that we have the imprint of death upon us, the mark of the cross, we do not wish to imply that henceforth we can neither speak nor work; it is only that we will not be so careless and self-reliant in both our speech and action. When a person is genuinely touched by God, being dealt with by the profound work of the cross, he becomes experientially weak and fearful and trembling, not in a debilitating way, but with a holy awe and dependence, with the result that he dares not confidently say "I can" or "I will do" in his own strength. He will still do his work, his ministry, his calling, yet now with the fear of God deeply in him, relying on His power. He will continue to walk his spiritual journey, only now he walks *after God*, step by step, just as Abraham walked step by step after God, not knowing precisely where he was going, but trusting the One who led him. In his life today, the mark of the cross is plainly noticeable, a divine piercing and breaking of the old self. He has been pierced by God; he is no longer intact in his self-sufficiency; he bears the indelible impress of death having worked in him, making way for resurrection life. This, this transformed existence bearing the mark of death overcome, is called resurrection.

If we genuinely know, experientially, what resurrection is, we will simultaneously know the cross as a profound, eliminating power in our lives. When we pass through the cross, allowing its work to have its effect, we will be rid of many things that once characterized our natural man.

Today, God, in His divine wisdom, communes with man in the realm of resurrection, and this resurrection, this new order of life, eternally includes the cross. Nothing, therefore, that is of our natural man, our fallen self, can be truly related to God, can have genuine spiritual value, without passing through death with Christ. All that is of the natural must go to death; its power must be broken. God cannot and will not contact or communicate on resurrection ground with anyone who has yet to die to themselves and be resurrected in Christ. We must experientially die with Him and then be resurrected by His life. The life we receive, the life that flows from Him, is resurrection life, a life that has passed through death and lives eternally. Everything we learn, everything we experience, everything we do which has any genuine relation to God must be raised from the dead, must bear the mark of resurrection.

In spiritual matters, we are often faced with one hard, persistent problem: that people often sincerely serve God with natural things, with their innate abilities, their human zeal, their own strength, instead of serving Him with resurrection things, with that which has passed through death and is animated by His life. Many have natural zeal, a human fervor, but tragically, few have resurrection zeal—a zeal which has gone through death, been broken at the cross, and is resurrected by the power of Christ, a zeal that is not of self but of God. Lots of natural zeal characterizes the first kind, often loud and demonstrative, but not the second, which is a quiet, profound fire from within. We observe a number of brethren working diligently and ably, using their natural talents, nonetheless their diligence and ability are often of the first kind—the natural—and not of the second, the resurrection kind, for they have not experientially passed through death in those areas. We cannot account it as genuine resurrection life or ministry if we live and serve before God in the power of these natural, un-crucified elements.

Some will sincerely ask, what is the body of Christ? The body of Christ, the Church, is the realm, the living organism, where the resurrection of Christ is genuinely attested, where His resurrection life is manifested and reigns. In other words, whatever is not of resurrection, whatever is of the natural man and has not passed through death with Christ, has no part, not even the slightest part, in the body of Christ; it is alien to its nature. The church is not the place where you bring in something of your human cleverness and I bring in something of my natural tactfulness, and together we build something. The church is not built by your contributing a little bit of some natural thing and my contributing a little bit of some other natural thing, a collection of human efforts. The church, in its divine essence, shuts all the natural out and accepts only the resurrected, only that which is born of God and bears the mark of the cross and resurrection. Whenever the natural enters, whenever human elements, the church loses its divine character, its spiritual power and witness. There can be no un-resurrected element, no un-crucified aspect of the natural man, in the true functioning of the church.

Many sincerely ask how the church can be one, how we can experience genuine unity. We ought to realize how futile it is to attempt to achieve true, spiritual unity through human ways, through organizational methods or external agreements. God's children need to experientially know the cross and to deal with the flesh and the natural man in order to arrive at genuine, spiritual oneness, a unity that is the product of His life, not our efforts. No human method is truly effective unless people experientially encounter Calvary, allowing the cross to do its work in their lives, breaking down the barriers of self and the natural. No problem in the church, no division, no conflict, is truly solved by human maneuver and ingenuity alone; these often exacerbate the issues. The church, in its divine constitution, allows neither the flesh nor the natural man to dominate or have sway, for both will inevitably damage her spiritual health and witness. It is quite true that the church requires the contributions and ministries of men and women, the exercise of their gifts and talents; nonetheless, there must be the indelible imprint of death upon them, a brokenness of self-reliance and a dependence on Christ. **Usefulness in the kingdom, accompanied by the mark of death, is called resurrection ministry**. The Lord Himself is resurrection, and He ardently desires to have a resurrection church, a body of believers who live and serve in the power of His resurrected life, bearing the marks of His cross.

Should we sincerely wish to have such a profound resurrection experience in our lives and in the church, then we must earnestly look to God for His deep, transformative working in our lives. Perhaps we are quite familiar with many teachings, many doctrines, yet without our receiving a basic, foundational blow from the Lord, a divine dealing with our natural man, we shall sadly remain essentially the same, unchanged in our core being. Sometimes we slip and fall, we make mistakes, and we feel the pain, yes; yet it only lasts a few days or a few months, and we recover, often returning to our old ways. But had we been given God's basic blow, His divine dealing, and been sufficiently broken at the cross, we would not be pained for merely a few days or a few months; we would sustain that spiritual wound, that mark of the cross, throughout our entire life. We would forever be, in a spiritual sense, "crippled" before God in our self-reliance, and the indelible mark of the cross would always be upon us, a constant reminder of our death to self and our dependence on Him.

We cannot account it as genuine resurrection life or ministry if we live and serve before God in the power of the natural, un-crucified elements.

Many years after the Apostle Paul had seen the blinding vision on the road to Damascus, a foundational blow that forever changed him, he testified with profound humility and conviction, **"Wherefore, O King Agrippa, I was not disobedient unto the heavenly vision"** (Acts 26:19, AMP). If the Lord, in His tender mercy, upon us and severely strikes us one day, dealing with our old selves at the cross, our old selves shall never be able to rise up again in their former strength; the wound, the mark of that divine dealing, will remain in us forever, a testament to His grace. Since it is still beautifully possible to touch, in the resurrected Christ, the wound of the nail prints in His hands and of the spear in His side, such wounding, such marks of having passed through death with

Him, should never disappear in the lives of all who today genuinely know the Lord as resurrection, as their life and triumph over death. Experiencing this wound, this brokenness of self, we will never more dare to boast of ourselves and of our own power; our confidence will be entirely in Christ. Once beaten by the Lord, once dealt with at the cross, we shall rise no more in our own strength; our old man is crucified with Him. May the marks of the cross, the evidence of His transformative work, be increasingly evident in our lives, a living testimony to His resurrection power.

Pretension, spiritual performance, is utterly useless here; it has no place in the realm of resurrection. For what is put on by oneself, a facade of spirituality, will soon be forgotten, fading away like a shadow. But once the sacrifice, our old self, is genuinely placed on the altar of the cross and slain with Christ, it never rises again in its former power; it is forever gone in death. If we have ever truly suffered this basic stroke, this divine dealing at the cross, we will realize with profound clarity how unable, how finished, how utterly "nothing" we are in ourselves, apart from Christ. This death mark in us, this brokenness of self, testifies to our genuine knowledge and experience of resurrection. Knowing the cross experientially is knowing resurrection; they are two sides of the same divine reality. What is left after the cross has done its work, after our old self has been dealt with, is resurrection life, Christ Himself living in us. Oh! How many are the things of our old nature, our pride, our self-will, our fallen desires, which shall never rise again but are forever gone once they have passed through the cross with Christ. Only what can endure the cross, only that which is of God and has His divine life, possesses true spiritual value and eternal significance. Whatever enters the grave of the cross and remains there is a dead thing, fit only for corruption; but whatever comes out on the other side of the grave, bearing the indelible mark of the cross, the evidence of death overcome, is resurrection, vibrant with the life of Christ.

Let us earnestly pray, with longing and sincere hearts, that we may truly know Christ to be our resurrection as well as our life, not just as a doctrine, but as a living, transformative reality. May the Lord, in His grace, eliminate many of our "things" from us, many aspects of our old nature and self-reliance. May He not only cause us to have more of His divine life flowing through us but also graciously grant us less of ourselves, less of our natural man. How often we, even as believers, live according to the natural, neither genuinely knowing God's loving discipline nor the profound work of the cross in our lives. We need to constantly ask the Lord to be merciful to us, to grant us His grace, that the natural, the un-crucified aspects of our being, may gradually be decreased in us while the resurrected, the life of Christ Himself, may be increasingly manifested through us. May life and resurrection be glorious realities—not just abstract theories—to us, shaping our every thought, word, and deed. Whenever we put forth our hand to serve or speak, may He graciously show us if there is no resurrection in it, no mark of the cross, since all that it performs is only natural and fleshly, a product of our old self. May He expose our flesh, our natural man, by the piercing light of resurrection, revealing what is not of Him. If we still cannot see, if we remain blind to these profound truths, may the Lord be merciful to us and grant us the spiritual seeing we so desperately need. So be it!

Let us Pray!

My God, I come to you with humble and open hands to receive the magnificent and complete gift of your Son, Jesus Christ, who is my Resurrection and my Life.

I acknowledge and receive the truth that my spiritual life is not about acquiring a collection of separate blessings or striving to achieve virtues, but solely about abiding in and possessing the Person of Christ Himself.

I receive the liberating reality that my old life is truly dead, and my new, real resurrection life is hidden securely with Christ in You, God. I thank you and receive the assurance that Christ is not merely the Giver of life, but that He is the very essence of all Life.

I receive the power to live victoriously right now. I receive Him as the living, ultimate Salvation itself, the Way I walk, the Truth that sets me free, and the divine, effortless wellspring of Life flowing through me every single moment.

I receive the fact that everything I need is embodied in Him—my Wisdom, my Righteousness, my Sanctification, and my Redemption.

I choose to stop striving to achieve and simply receive the glorious Person of Jesus Christ, who is my complete Everything.

Amen.

5

The Bread and Light of Life

Jesus told them, "**I am the Bread of Life; whoever comes to Me will not hunger, and whoever believes in** (adheres to, trusts in, relies on) **Me will never thirst**" (John 6:35, AMP).

Again, Jesus spoke to them, saying, "**I am the Light of the world; he who follows Me will not walk in darkness,** but will have the Light of [eternal] life" (John 8:12, AMP).

We've explored the profound truth that all spiritual realities are deeply rooted and found in Christ Himself. God, in His infinite wisdom and boundless love, has graciously given us His Son to embody and encompass every single one of these divine truths. This isn't just a theological concept; it's a foundational and absolutely crucial point for truly understanding and navigating our spiritual journey. It prompts us to ask ourselves a series of deeply reflective questions: Is our spiritual experience merely a collection of isolated events or fleeting emotions, or is it fundamentally about Christ living and moving within us? Is the righteousness we strive for simply an outward adherence to rules, or is it the very righteousness of Christ imputed to us and actively expressed through our lives? Is our sanctification laborious self-improvement project, or is it Christ, who *is* holy, continually transforming us from the inside out? And finally, is our redemption just a past event of being saved from sin, or is it Christ, our Redeemer, actively and continually setting us free and making us whole in every aspect of our being?

Often, we talk about "the way," but that way might not be Christ Himself. Similarly, we can discuss profound concepts like truth and life without necessarily referring to Christ as their ultimate source and embodiment. In short, we frequently find ourselves accumulating many spiritual "things" that are, in essence, separate from Christ. This creates a significant spiritual challenge for God's children, as it can lead to a fragmented and less powerful faith experience. We might readily confess with our mouths that Christ is the absolute center of everything—the Alpha and the Omega—yet in our daily lives, we inadvertently rely on a multitude of other things, believing, perhaps subtly, that these can somehow help us to truly live out our calling as Christians.

Christ is not merely the dispenser of these blessings; He is the very essence of them. For He is the totality, the sum, and the complete embodiment of all spiritual realities.

We desperately need our minds to be renewed by the Holy Spirit so we can grasp that, apart from Christ, God doesn't intend for us to have a collection of so-called spiritual "things" that operate independently. According to God's divine and perfect plan, there are indeed "things" that are essential for our spiritual walk, but these "things" *are* Christ Himself. He is not merely the dispenser of these blessings; He *is* the very essence of them. For Christ is the totality, the sum, and the complete embodiment of all spiritual realities. Consider this: Christ *is* our righteousness—He hasn't just given us a separate, external righteousness to put on. Christ *is* our sanctification—He hasn't merely granted us a power or a method to make us holy; He *is* our holiness, continually working within us. Christ *is* our redemption—He hasn't simply offered us a redemption as a transaction; He *is* our Redeemer, the very act and ongoing reality of our freedom. Christ *is* the way—He hasn't just opened up another path for us to walk; He *is* the living, dynamic path itself. Christ *is* the truth—He hasn't just presented some truth for us to understand intellectually; He *is* the living, liberating truth that transforms us. And profoundly, Christ *is* the life—He hasn't just conferred upon us a thing called life; He *is* our very spiritual existence, vibrant and eternal. This understanding shifts our focus from striving for disconnected spiritual attributes to embracing the Person of Christ as our all-sufficient source.

As we journey along God's path, we will increasingly discover that among all of God's grace, there is only one grace, and among all of God's gifts, there is only one gift. That grace is Christ, and that gift is also Christ. Thank God, day after day He is revealing to us how Christ is all-encompassing. Previously, we thought of the Lord as our Savior; now we can declare that He is not only our Savior but also our very salvation. Does this seem strange to you? No, this is a profound reality. For we are continually uncovering that Christ *is* the very essence of God's provision.

If we mistakenly separate what the Lord Jesus gives from what He *is*—the gift from the Giver—we will suffer greatly in our spiritual lives. Such an error will prevent us from truly connecting with the source of life. With this in mind, we desire to see more of Christ as our all-encompassing "things." In John 6:35 and 8:12, the Lord tells us that He is the Bread of Life and also the Light of Life. Let's explore each of these in turn.

It's a beautiful journey of faith to truly grasp this foundational truth: every spiritual blessing, every divine attribute, every aspect of our walk with God is not a separate "thing" given *by* Christ, but is profoundly *Christ Himself* dwelling within us. When we talk about our experience of God, it's not just a series of events or feelings; it's Christ living and moving in us. Our righteousness isn't merely a status we achieve; its Christ's perfect righteousness imputed to us and expressed through us. Our sanctification isn't just a process of becoming holy; it's Christ, who *is* holy, making us like Himself. Our redemption isn't just a past event of being saved; it's Christ, our Redeemer, continually setting us free and making us whole.

The challenge we often face as God's children is that we tend to compartmentalize our faith, seeking individual "spiritual things" outside of the all-sufficient Person of Christ. We might chase after methods, doctrines, or experiences, hoping they will fill a void, when all along, Christ Himself is the complete answer. Our minds desperately need to be renewed by the Holy Spirit to fully comprehend that God's divine intention is for Christ to be *everything* to us. There are indeed "things" in God's plan, but these "things" are not separate from Christ; they *are* Christ in His fullness. He is the sum total of all spiritual realities, the ultimate embodiment of every grace and gift.

This profound revelation transforms our perspective. We don't just receive grace *from* Christ; Christ *is* our grace. We don't just receive gifts *from* Him; Christ *is* the ultimate gift. Day after day, as we walk with Him, the Holy Spirit lovingly unveils how truly all-encompassing Christ is. We once saw Him as our Savior, and indeed He is! But now, we can declare with even greater joy that He is not only our Savior but also our very salvation—the entire process and reality of being saved. This isn't strange; it's a glorious, liberating fact! We are continually discovering that Christ *is* the very essence of God's boundless provision for us, meeting our every need and exceeding our every expectation. When we truly embrace this, our spiritual lives flourish, and we connect with the inexhaustible source of life itself.

Christ Is the Bread of Life

"I am the Bread of Life; whoever comes to Me will not hunger, and whoever believes in (adheres to, trusts in, relies on) Me will never thirst" (John 6:35, AMP).

The Lord declares, "I am the bread of life." He spoke these powerful words to people in Capernaum who were seeking Him, expecting Him to feed them with physical bread. But Jesus, in His profound wisdom, revealed a deeper truth: "I am the bread of life." He is not just the one who *gives* the bread of life; He *is* that bread. What a glorious reality—the gift and the Giver are one, perfectly united! Thank God, Christ is both God's ultimate gift and the Lord who graciously provides it.

What does "bread" signify in the Bible? It beautifully represents satisfaction, as Scripture often uses the metaphor of hunger to illustrate the deep human dissatisfaction that can plague our souls. For our deepest human longings—our spiritual hunger—to be truly met, we need this divine "bread." This isn't just a metaphor; it points to a fundamental need within us.

Whether God's children possess the strength to persevere

through life's challenges and ultimately finish their spiritual journey depends significantly on their inner satisfaction. If we feel truly satisfied and nourished in our spirit today, we will possess the necessary strength and resilience for the day ahead. Conversely, if we sense an inner emptiness, a profound void much like a deflated balloon, we might struggle immensely to carry on, feeling depleted and without purpose. It's not that spiritual life is entirely absent in such moments, but rather that this inexplicable, profound feeling of satisfaction is what truly empowers us to move forward, to endure, and to complete the divine course set before us.

Christ is not just the one who gives the bread of life; He is that bread. What a glorious reality—the gift and the Giver are one, perfectly united!

So, what is this "bread" for God's children? The Lord Jesus Himself declares, "I am the bread of life." This profound statement reveals that the Lord Jesus not only sustains our spiritual life but also *is* that very life, the source and essence of it. Many Christians often limit their understanding of spiritual nourishment to practices like an hour of prayer or an hour of Bible reading. While these are indeed wonderful and vital spiritual disciplines, they sometimes miss the profound, overarching truth that their ultimate and most essential "food" is the Lord Jesus Himself. We are not suggesting that prayer or Bible reading are unimportant; rather, we emphasize the Lord Jesus's emphatic declaration: He *is* "the bread of life"—meaning the life-giving divine food, the very essence of spiritual sustenance, is none other than the Lord Himself! He is the living, dynamic provision for every spiritual need.

Often, God's children feel unsatisfied because they haven't fully grasped Christ as the bread of life. We frequently encounter individuals who are spiritually hungry and discontent. They seem unhappy with everything, from morning till night, consumed by dissatisfaction. We certainly don't want to encourage arrogance or self-contentment. However, we believe there's a clear distinction between prideful self-satisfaction and being genuinely fed and content in Christ. Some individuals, having been deeply touched by God, live before Him in humility and reverence. They have not the slightest hint of pride, yet they have truly connected with the Lord, and in doing so, they are completely nourished. They possess a profound satisfaction in God's presence, and this satisfaction becomes their strength.

How, then, can we be fully fed and satisfied? We must understand that all true satisfaction is intimately connected to Christ. All genuine fulfillment is found in life itself. Christ is the bread of life! Whenever we truly connect with this divine life, we immediately experience deep satisfaction. Conversely, when we act against this life, we instantly feel a spiritual "blow-out" or emptiness, a profound sense of depletion that hinders our spiritual progress. Let's illustrate this profound truth of obtaining satisfaction with some practical examples from Scripture and everyday experience.

Imagine someone saying, "I've been working for over a year now, keeping incredibly busy, running here and there, constantly engaged in various activities. I've been so swamped that I now feel completely empty inside, utterly drained of spiritual vitality. I'm spiritually hungry and long for a place of revival, a source of renewed strength and purpose." This sentiment is common among those who strive in their own strength. However, in John Chapter 4, we find a beautiful contrast to this sentiment in the life of Jesus. The Lord Jesus, weary from His journey, sat by Jacob's well. His disciples had gone into the city to buy food, suggesting the Lord was indeed physically hungry. There, He met a Samaritan woman. It was God's divine will that He speak to her and bring her salvation, a task He faithfully embraced. He did precisely what God willed Him to do. When His disciples returned with food, they urged Him to eat. But He told them, "I have food to eat which you do not know about." They, naturally, thought someone else had brought Him food, failing to grasp the deeper spiritual reality. Consequently, He plainly revealed to them, "**My food is to do the will of Him who sent Me and to completely finish His work**" (John 4:34, AMP). This powerful declaration highlights that true spiritual nourishment comes not from physical sustenance or human effort, but from aligning with and fulfilling God's divine will.

From this powerful incident in the life of our Lord, we can joyfully conclude that true spiritual work should *fill* us, not leave us empty and hungry! In genuine spiritual labor, every time we serve, we should feel a sense of fullness. If hunger consistently follows our work, something might be amiss. If, after laboring, we feel weak, it indicates an issue with that particular effort. For if we walk according to God's will and not in our own strength, we should feel strengthened, not depleted. How often we undertake tasks, not because we are truly prepared before the Lord, but because the external need seems overwhelming or outside persuasion is strong. In such endeavors, we experience an inner shattering that leaves us drained after the work. This is a clear sign that something is not right between us and the Lord. All labors undertaken outside of God's will ultimately lead to greater spiritual hunger. Therefore, we must diligently do God's will to experience true satisfaction.

It's a wonderful realization that neither a powerful spiritual retreat nor a deep Biblical teaching, in themselves, are our ultimate source of sustenance; Christ alone is our true and complete food! If Christ is indeed our spiritual nourishment, then we must re-evaluate the idea that working until exhaustion, only to then seek replenishment at a retreat, is the full answer to our spiritual needs. Similarly, we shouldn't feel depleted after sharing our faith, only to then desperately seek new teachings to refill our spiritual reserves.

True spiritual nourishment comes not from physical sustenance or human effort, but from aligning with and fulfilling God's divine will.

Instead, whether we are actively engaged in ministry or simply navigating our daily lives, every time we rise to speak for Christ, we should be so overflowing with His words and inner strength that not only are those who hear us deeply fed, but we ourselves are also profoundly sustained! This is because it is the Lord Himself who works powerfully within us. When we truly connect with Him, we won't feel empty upon completing our tasks, but rather a deep and abiding fullness will settle within our hearts.

It's a beautiful truth to embrace that we are often mistaken if we regard mere rest, or simply listening to a sermon, or participating in a spiritual retreat as the *sole* means of being filled up. To obtain true, life-giving food and spiritual nourishment is to humbly allow the Lord to work out in us whatever He desires to accomplish. The Lord who graciously dwells within us empowers us to touch His very life, and this intimate connection alone causes us to feel profoundly and eternally full within, ready to face any challenge with His strength and joy.

In spiritual experience, it is not the leisurely who truly "eat"; on the contrary, we eat *more* when we are actively engaged! We are nourished as we are busily occupied. If we are walking in the will of God, the more we are busy, the more we spiritually "eat." And consequently, we will not be exhausted or feel empty through much toil.

"But those who wait for the Lord [who expect, look for, and hope in Him] **Will gain new strength and renew their power; They will lift up their wings** [and rise up close to God] **like eagles [rising toward the sun]; They will run and not become weary, They will walk and not grow tired"** (Isaiah 40:31 AMP).

Many of you can undoubtedly bear witness to this. Imagine, for example, a day when you enthusiastically go out to share with another person, speaking with great passion and conviction. Yet, despite your earnest efforts, you sense no divine movement or anointing flowing through you. After just five or ten minutes, to your genuine surprise, you begin to feel an unsettling sense that something is amiss. You soon find yourself wishing to change the direction of your conversation, realizing with a growing unease that you simply cannot continue as before. The disheartening result is that you feel utterly empty and drained when you eventually walk away. Outwardly, there might have been nothing wrong with your words or your attitude; you truly tried your very best to help that person. Yet, strangely, you became emptier and more depleted as you continued to speak. When you finally had to leave, a heavy sense of burden settled upon you, almost as if you had committed a sin. At times, you might even have observed a little outward success, or perhaps had the fleeting feeling that you had done quite well; nevertheless, when these external feelings inevitably pass away, you are left with a profound sense of emptiness and spiritual hunger inside. How true it is that whenever you move forward in your own strength, relying solely on your own abilities, despite some degree of outward success, you will eventually feel like a punctured balloon, deflated and without spiritual vitality.

Have you ever felt as though you had run completely out of spiritual air, lacking the very breath of God's life within you? If you walk according to your own thoughts, relying on your own wisdom and understanding, instead of humbly and reverently following the Lord with a deep sense of dependence, however good and well-intentioned your efforts may be, you will always end up feeling depleted—lacking true spiritual punch and power. The more you labor in your own strength, the less meaningful and fulfilling it becomes to you. The more you continue on this path, the emptier and more weary you feel. In such a challenging situation, you will often feel even worse if you receive praise from others, as it highlights the internal disconnect you experience. You might even find yourself disliking your own efforts. This clearly demonstrates that such work, though perhaps well-intentioned, is not true spiritual food, as it fails to genuinely satisfy the deepest longings of your soul. But take heart, for there is a better way—a way of abiding in Christ, our true and inexhaustible source of life and satisfaction.

Despite our best intentions, it is only when we genuinely align ourselves with and follow the Lord's leading that we achieve profound and lasting satisfaction.

Consider another, though deeper, instance that illuminates this principle. Oftentimes, we find ourselves doing what we genuinely believe to be good and spiritual, yet we proceed without truly discerning the Lord's mind or will for that situation. Consequently, a feeling of emptiness often follows, leaving us unfulfilled despite our best intentions. It is only when we genuinely align ourselves with and follow the Lord's leading that we achieve profound and lasting satisfaction.

Let us uncover an important and liberating fact: that the "good" which one can perform merely from their own natural strength, their human will, or their self-conceived gentleness, is not true spiritual food. You might intellectually conclude that it would be better to be more gentle or strong in a given situation, yet spiritual experience repeatedly tells us that even if you act in a gentle or strong manner from your outward man—your natural self—this action, however commendable in appearance, cannot provide genuine spiritual nourishment. True, lasting nourishment and profound satisfaction come only when the Lord Himself moves within you, and you, in turn, move in complete accordance with His divine will. As you truly touch His life, you receive spiritual food; as you genuinely touch the Lord, you are profoundly and completely satisfied.

Christ Is the Light of Life

The Lord doesn't just refer to Himself as "the bread of life"; He also powerfully states, "I am the light of life." Think of it this way: bread is all about satisfying our hunger and providing nourishment, while light is essential for us to see clearly and navigate our surroundings. Just as satisfaction gives us the energy and strength to keep going, seeing clearly directly impacts how we walk through life. We've already explored the profound meaning of Christ as the bread of life, and now we'll delve into what it means for Him to be the light of life.

It's crucial to understand from the outset that this "light of life" isn't simply about having a vast knowledge of the Bible. Of course, every Christian knows the importance of diligently reading and studying their Scriptures. However, if we approach the Bible merely as a source of intellectual knowledge or a theological textbook, that's precisely what we'll get—just information. We might become incredibly familiar with various biblical doctrines, even accurate ones, but these remain just words on a page, without truly transforming us. Consider the time when Jesus was born in Bethlehem; many priests and scribes were deeply versed in the prophetic books, yet they failed to recognize the very Christ those prophecies foretold. Today, with the New Testament added to the Old, it's still entirely possible for people to memorize every letter of the Bible and yet not genuinely know Christ in a living, personal way. We are certainly not suggesting that reading the Scriptures is unnecessary; rather, we are emphasizing that it's possible to gain a great deal of knowledge from the Word without ever truly encountering Christ Himself through it.

In Christ's time, many religious leaders, priests, and scribes possessed what could be described as a "dead knowledge"—they had intellectual understanding but lacked a vibrant, living relationship with the Lord. Unfortunately, many people today still make the mistake of equating mere knowledge, doctrine, theology, or teaching with the true light of life. Some might even claim to have been "enlightened," but what they perceive as light might only be a particular interpretation of a Scripture passage or a specific teaching about the Bible. The real light, however, is far more than just knowledge or intellectual insight. It is none other than the Lord Jesus Christ Himself. He emphatically declares, "I am the light of life," signifying that He is the living, illuminating source that guides us, not just a collection of facts or theories. This light enables us to see spiritual truths, understand God's will, and walk in His ways with clarity and purpose, far beyond what any amount of academic study alone can provide.

In Christ's time, many religious leaders, priests, and scribes possessed what could be described as a "dead knowledge"—they had intellectual understanding but lacked a vibrant, living relationship with the Lord.

Our experience as believers is that what we genuinely perceive in the light of life is often something so deep and transformative that we struggle to put it into words. It might seem strange that we can "see" something so clearly, yet find ourselves unable to fully articulate it. Consider as an example the story of a person who was once asked if she was saved. Her simple yet powerful reply was, "Yes, I am newly saved, yet I don't know how to explain it. But I do know I am saved. If you believe I am saved, I am saved; even if you do not believe I am saved, still I am saved." Her words resonated with authenticity. She had experienced a genuine spiritual transformation, a deep inner knowing, but the intellectual framework to explain it wasn't immediately available to her. This is often our experience, we know that we know because we have seen it in the light. Words for it may never come.

So, what exactly is the profound difference between seeing this light and not seeing it? What kind of radical transformation occurs within us when we truly encounter it? The distinction is immense, truly monumental. If we have genuinely seen this divine light, the immediate and often overwhelming effect is that we are brought low; we "fall to the ground," so to speak. This is because this light not only illuminates our understanding but also has a "slaying" effect on our pride, our self-sufficiency, and our old ways of thinking. Think of the Apostle Paul's dramatic conversion on the road to Damascus. Before that powerful encounter with the light of Christ, it would have been incredibly difficult to humble him or cause him to yield. Yet, as soon as he was struck by that intense light, he was instantly flung to the ground, utterly undone by its power.

Some individuals, in their earnest desire for spiritual growth, might try to force themselves into humility. Their words may sound humble, their manners may appear modest, but this kind of self-imposed humility is often incredibly exhausting—both for them and for those around them. It's like a small child attempting to learn all the words of a big dictionary: even if the book isn't physically heavy, the sheer effort required drains the child's strength. How incredibly difficult it is for the proud heart to genuinely become humble! How challenging it is for us to step down from the "throne of pride" we often build for ourselves! But when the pure, unadulterated light of the Lord truly shines into our lives, we are instantly leveled. We may not intellectually grasp *how* it happens, but we instinctively understand that this divine light inherently brings us to a place of profound humility and dependence on God. It strips away our self-reliance and exposes the true condition of our hearts, leaving us with nothing but a deep awareness of His majesty and our need for Him.

We may not intellectually grasp how it happens, but we instinctively understand that the light of the Lord inherently brings us to a place of profound humility and dependence on God.

Doctrine, in itself, doesn't inherently cause anyone to stumble or fall. One might diligently listen to numerous messages, even committing them to memory, yet their inner being remains unchanged. They can approach a profound message that ought to stir their emotions to tears, or a powerful word meant to shatter their self-centered life, as nothing more than a weekly ritual. In such unfortunate instances, doctrine, teaching, and even the very Word of God become mere "things"—intellectual concepts devoid of spiritual vitality. These are essentially dead; there is no genuine light radiating from them to bring about true transformation.

This divine light is incredibly potent and rigorous. It possesses the power to accomplish what human effort alone cannot. What intellectual doctrine fails to achieve, what the well-intentioned help of others cannot bring about, and what our own strenuous efforts fall short of, this light can immediately and miraculously accomplish. We might perceive ourselves as hard-hearted or resistant to change, but when the light of the Lord shines upon us, we are supernaturally softened and made pliable. Think of John, who, upon encountering this light, became "as one dead" (Revelation 1:17); Daniel had a similar experience. No one is truly able to behold the glorious face of the Lord without being brought low, without falling down in awe and reverence. It is incredibly difficult for our proud human nature to "die" to self, and it is a monumental challenge for us to genuinely embrace humility.

However, as soon as this divine light shines, these seemingly impossible transformations occur effortlessly. The light that emanates from the Lord carries a "slaying power." It brings people to their knees, not in a destructive way, but in a way that dismantles their self-sufficiency and opens them up to God's transformative grace.

The Lord Jesus Himself is the light. Consequently, anyone who truly encounters Him is profoundly affected, often feeling overwhelmed and humbled, as if brought to the brink of spiritual death. Many individuals possess a naturally strong, unyielding character; they've never been truly broken or softened by the Lord, and neither they nor anyone else seems capable of dealing with their stubbornness. However, when the radiant light of the Lord shines upon them, something remarkable happens. As soon as they perceive this light, their tough exterior begins to crack, and they become "broken vessels," ready to be reshaped by God. A person who genuinely sees the Lord is undeniably weakened in their self-reliance and deeply humbled. It's as if their old way of living becomes impossible after beholding His glory. This, in its transformative power, is what we mean by "light."

David's perspective of the Lord was that He is the one who brings light into his darkness. The key in David's life wasn't his brightness, it was his dependance.

"For You cause my lamp **to be lighted** and to shine; the Lord my God **illumines** my darkness" (Psalm 18:28 AMP).

The very first and most profound effect of this divine light is to "slay"—to dismantle our self-sufficiency and pride. Don't mistakenly believe that light comes solely to enable us to see clearly from the outset. That's not entirely the case. When this powerful light truly dawns upon us, its initial impact is often to "blind" our natural eyes, or at least to daze us. While it does indeed cause us to see, this is a subsequent effect, following the initial humbling. The light first overwhelms us and prostrates us before it ever truly enables us to perceive spiritual realities with clarity. Anything that we say we received from the Lord that cannot bring us to our knees, that does not profoundly humble us, is not the true light of Christ. Remember Paul's experience: when he saw the light, he was immediately struck to the ground and remained blind for three days. Therefore, during our initial encounter with this light, we are likely to be dazed, disoriented, and profoundly impacted. The moment someone who has been dwelling in spiritual darkness beholds this light, they will find their old way of seeing, and indeed their old way of being, completely disrupted.

 May God have mercy upon those who are so deeply entrenched in self-righteousness and self-conceit. Such individuals, sadly, have never truly encountered the illuminating power of divine light; all they possess are mere doctrines and intellectual knowledge. If they had truly seen the genuine light, their immediate and heartfelt confession would be, "Oh Lord, what do I *really* know?! I know absolutely nothing in and of myself!" This illustrates a profound spiritual principle: the greater the revelation of God's light, **the deeper our awareness of our own spiritual blindness**; the stronger the light shines, the more severe the "stroke" it delivers to our pride and self-sufficiency.

It's vital to grasp that light is not an abstract concept; it is something incredibly substantial and real. The Lord Jesus Himself is that light. With Him dwelling among us and within us, we have true light in our midst.

This divine light will humble us and bring us to our knees *before* it ever truly enables us to see with spiritual clarity. If we haven't been profoundly smitten, humbled, dazed, and ultimately reduced to a state of utter dependence on God, it serves as undeniable proof that we are still dwelling in spiritual darkness, possessing no true light. May the Lord, in His boundless mercy, shine His light upon us so powerfully that it strips away our self-reliance, preventing us from ever daring to trust in our own limited knowledge and flawed judgment again. Oh, that we may come to Him with hearts wide open, declaring, "Lord, You are the light. In seeing You, I now realize that everything I once considered 'truth' or 'understanding' in the past were merely 'things'—abstract concepts, not the living reality of Your presence."

It's vital to grasp that light is not an abstract concept; it is something incredibly substantial and real. The Lord Jesus Himself *is* that light. With Him dwelling among us and within us, we have true light in our midst. It's truly regrettable how many aspects of believers' lives remain purely theoretical. They have heard countless abstract teachings and concepts that, while perhaps intellectually stimulating, offer very little practical help or transformative power in their daily lives.

Why is it that after a few days, the profound truths of God we hear seem to lose their power, becoming so weak that they no longer deeply touch or transform us? There is no other reason than this: it has become too much doctrine, too much theological knowledge, without the living presence of Christ! Let's consider holiness for example. After hearing many discussions on the concept of holiness, I may decide to dive deeply into the doctrine of holiness. I may meticulously search the New Testament and find over two hundred verses on the subject. I memorize each one and carefully arrange them in a systematic order. Despite all this intellectual effort, I still not *knowing* what holiness is; and I will probably feel a profound emptiness inside. This feeling of spiritual void will persist because holiness is not a disembodied knowledge. But if one day I meet someone who genuinely embodied holiness, my spiritual eyes will be opened to truly *see* what holiness is, because I had encountered a person who was holy. The light of this kind of revelation is overwhelming, almost terrible in its intensity, because the light will pierce me through. It may cause me immense inner pain, offering no escape from its truth. It unequivocally showed me what holiness truly is. I could say then that the Lord brought light into my darkness (unholiness in this case) and I could see clearly.

We desperately need to recognize that **only the living Lord can truly beget living people**. We should earnestly pray for God to be merciful to us, enabling us more and more to see that all "things"—all spiritual concepts, practices, and even gifts, if separated from Christ—are ultimately dead. It is the Lord alone who is living, vibrant, and eternally active. Even the most attractive and seemingly spiritual aspects of Christianity, if they exist outside of a living connection with Christ, are but lifeless forms. We must allow the Lord Himself to *be* this thing or that thing to us. Then, and only then, does it become truly living—alive both within us and in those who receive from us. May the Lord be gracious to us, bringing us to a place of profound humility before Him, where we can truly know Him in a way that transcends mere intellectual understanding.

"The people who walk in [spiritual] **darkness will see a great Light; those who live in the dark land, the Light will shine on them"** (Isaiah 9:2 AMP).

Father God, we come to you today with hearts overflowing with celebration for the glorious truth of your Son, Jesus Christ, who is the Bread of our Life and the Light of our World! We celebrate that you have given us nothing less than Christ Himself, and that He is not merely a provider, but the very essence of all we need.

We celebrate that Jesus declares, "I am the Bread of Life." We no longer strive to find spiritual nourishment or chase after temporary satisfaction, for we receive Him as the life-sustaining essence that completely satisfies our souls.

We celebrate that Jesus also proclaims, "I am the Light of the world." We rejoice that He is not just able to give us light, but that He is the very source and essence of all divine light and truth. We celebrate that in following Him, we are eternally freed from walking in darkness and now have the eternal Light of life shining from within us.

We celebrate the profound reality that in our lives, the focus is never on external "things" or abstract concepts, but solely on the living Person of Christ. We celebrate that you have opened our spiritual eyes to see that Christ is our All in All, the one in whom all good, true, and virtuous reality resides. We thank you for transforming our spiritual journey from religious striving into simply receiving and enjoying a relationship with the Person who is everything.

In the mighty name of Jesus, our Bread and our Light, we celebrate You. Amen!

6

It's All About a Person

You might wonder why we focus so heavily on this one essential point, but understanding it is the difference between a thriving, **Living Christianity** and a draining, formulaic one. The gap between these two approaches is immense, almost beyond measure. One is vibrant, spiritual, and divine, flowing from the heart of God; the other is often just a humanly-designed system of effort and invention. When you study the Bible with an open heart, you'll discover this profound truth: the entire narrative revolves around a single, glorious **Person**, not a collection of fragmented spiritual things or abstract concepts. That Person is the Lord Jesus Christ, and in Him, you have the complete picture.

A major challenge for believers today is that their view of faith can be fragmented, like a patchwork quilt of separate pieces. We often hear a Christian life described by its parts: "I got a little grace," "I have a specific spiritual gift," "I'm working on patience," or "She has a measure of humility." This becomes what is often called Christianity. But is it? No. **Christianity is Christ Himself**. It is not a reward to be earned, nor is it merely a list of gifts that Christ gives to me. Christianity is nothing less than the dynamic, personal presence of Christ in my life.

Do you see the critical, life-altering distinction? These are two entirely different paths. Christianity is not about receiving an isolated item from Christ; it is about Christ giving Himself to me completely and without reserve. The modern struggle is that many believers treat Christianity as a spiritual endowment. We think: "When I was a sinner, Christ endowed me with mercy. Now that I'm a Christian, He endows me with patience, then humility, then gentleness," and so on, as if these are separate virtues to be collected. But the truth is far more glorious and simpler.

Embracing the Personal Nature of Faith

Before God, this whole matter is not about the endowment of spiritual qualities, but about **God giving Christ Himself to us**. He hasn't just granted you humility, patience, or gentleness as separate traits; He has granted you the **entirety of Christ**. It is the living Lord Jesus who becomes your humility, your patience, and your gentleness. This is the very essence of what is truly called Christianity.

It is vital to recognize that there is absolutely nothing impersonal in the Christian life. Every single element of your walk with God is personal because the Person involved is Christ. To put it another way, let's reframe those spiritual terms we often treat as "things":

- Your **Patience** is not a thing; your patience is a **Person**.
- Your **Sanctification** is not an experience or a process; your sanctification is a **Man**.
- Your **Justification** is not an abstract declaration; your

justification is a **Personality**.

- Your **Righteousness** is not perfect behavior; your righteousness is a **Being**.

When we are saved and delivered, we don't obtain a list of items; our redemption, deliverance, patience, humility, and love are all the Lord Himself—they are not things. This is the liberated, genuine reality of Christianity. In a true believer's life, Christ is already the all-inclusive answer, and we don't need to wait for a future day to experience this fullness.

Many people will naturally ask, how can we possibly say Christ is all? The answer is simple: if you have truly grasped the relational core of a living Christianity, you will effortlessly acknowledge that Christ is all. It's not that He gives all things; it's that **He is all things.**

A common struggle and a major source of defeat for God's children is this very confusion. They are focused on acquiring the gift instead of embracing the One that gives it. They seek fragmented spiritual items but miss the Christ of God entirely. They possess objects and things (a rule, a practice, a doctrine) but not the all-sufficient **Person**. Gaining this single, vital perspective—that Christ is all—is the solution that resolves every other problem in the spiritual life.

The entire narrative of the Bible revolves around a single, glorious Person, not a collection of abstract concepts. That Person is the Lord Jesus Christ, and in Him, you have the complete picture.

Consider the moment you were saved. You heard the glorious

message of John 3:16, that "God so loved the world, that he gave his only begotten Son, that whosoever believeth on him should not perish, but have eternal life." You felt your need for salvation and sincerely prayed. But how often do believers still go to God and plead, "Lord, you are my Savior, but will you now *also* give me salvation?" It seems foolish to ask for the product when you have the Source, as if the Savior Himself is not enough. Yet, many still do this in so many ways.

The gospel we preach is that God has given us the Savior. The truth we must grasp in prayer is this: **God has one Son, and this Son is your salvation.** In possessing the Savior, you already possess salvation. Why beg for the latter when you have the former? It is the height of liberation to realize that since you have embraced the Savior, you have everything.

This is the reason why God reveals that Christ's very name is **"I AM."** This name is not just a description of His power; it is the ultimate promise of His completeness. He is not just the one who *will* provide; He is the Self-Existing, All-Sufficient One who **is** the answer to every need you will ever face. We are invited, even urged, to understand and experience the liberating fullness of this blessed name in our daily walk.

Receiving the Living Sustenance

The Lord Jesus makes a remarkable declaration in the Gospel of John: "I am the bread of life." Yet, in our human hunger, we often miss the significance of this statement. We approach Him asking for "bread," treating it as a simple commodity or an item on a spiritual shopping list. We feel the deep, empty ache within and earnestly plead with God to just give us *something* to fill it, *some kind of food* if it's His will.

It is a truly astonishing discovery to realize that often, those who are only begging for the impersonal "bread" never receive it in the form they expect, and as a result, their deepest hunger persists. This raises a natural question: are God's promises somehow faulty? Doesn't the Scripture assure us that "he satisfieth the longing soul, and the hungry soul he filleth with good" (Psalm 107:9) and that "the hungry he hath filled with good things" (Luke 1:53)? Absolutely, God's Word is true!

The powerful key lies in understanding *what* those "good things" truly are. The profound truth that satisfies us completely before God is not an abstract concept or a mere physical provision; it is Christ Himself.

How frequently do we feel that spiritual emptiness, believing God has the supply and expecting some tangible "food" to materialize from our prayer? We often don't know the exact mechanism for receiving this nourishment. All we truly need to do is keep drawing near to the Lord, trusting and accepting more of Him, and simply enjoying His presence.

The beautiful surprise is this: even when the specific "food" we imagined doesn't appear, we find ourselves profoundly and wholly satisfied. We don't get the item we mentally requested, but our nearness to the Lord provides a supernatural fulfillment. We are satisfied by fully believing in and accepting *Him.*

There is a profound and life-changing reason for my constant joy and endless praise to God: my righteousness is not a set of rules, a record of my own performance, or a fleeting feeling. It is a living, breathing **Person**: the Lord Jesus Christ Himself. This truth is incredibly liberating and foundational to our faith! Think about the sheer wonder of this: because my righteousness is the Lord Jesus, it means I don't just *possess* a good standing with God; I have a dynamic *relationship* with my standing. I can actually speak to my righteousness! I can praise Him, give glory to Him, and thank Him because He is my very perfection, freely given. You might pause and wonder, "How can you praise your righteousness?" I can do it every day, because my righteousness is not an abstract concept or a "thing" I earned—it is the glorious Person of Christ, the One who is everything.

This same principle applies to my holiness, which is equally outside the realm of my own fragile behavior. My holiness is not the result of my strenuous, daily striving or an impressive display of disciplined behavior. I can praise my holiness, but for sure I am *not* praising my own conduct! My personal actions often fall short, and I detest the shortcomings of my old nature. But I can shout praises to my holiness because my holiness is also my **Lord**. He dwells within me, and *His* perfect, pure life is the holiness I celebrate.

This is the glorious and radical distinction of the Christian life. We are contrasting two utterly opposite realities: on one side, there is an inanimate **thing**—our weak human effort, a set of doctrines, or a list of good behaviors. On the other side is the **Lord**—a vibrant, living, all-sufficient Person. When Christ is our Righteousness and Holiness, everything flows with divine life and effortlessness, giving us an unshakeable confidence and an endless source of praise. It's not about *doing* the Christian life; it's about *beholding* and *receiving* Him who is everything to us.

God's Process of Refining and Rebuilding

It's a surprisingly common and often bewildering fact of the spiritual life: many of us find that after years—even decades—of being Christians, we struggle with the very things we seemed to master easily in the beginning. We hear from fellow believers how, early on, they were naturally able to be patient, quick to forgive, and consistent in prayer. They could handle tough situations at school, at home, or in the workplace with a surprising amount of grace. But now? Now, they confess they just can't seem to sustain it. Even if they manage to hold back a full-blown outburst, the inward thought of resentment or even a desire for payback can be a constant struggle. These stories are everywhere. It's disheartening to find that the humility, patience, gentleness, love, and zeal that once seemed so readily available are now difficult to access or have simply faded away.

If you've experienced this, take heart—this unexpected decline in your natural goodness is often a sign of God's deeper, more glorious work in your life.

Here is a vital truth to hold onto: **God must gently but firmly remove every *thing* that isn't Christ.**

When we first came to the Lord, we recognized a need, perhaps for love in a difficult relationship. So, we asked God for love, and in a sense, He graciously gave us a 'starter kit'—a measure of love to help us begin. In that moment, love was like an external gift, an *object* we possessed. But here is the critical point: God's ultimate desire is not for you to simply have a *bag of love* forever. He is determined to make **Christ Himself your love.** And to achieve this, He has to eventually allow that initial, personal 'thing' or 'object' called love to be taken away.

The same pattern applies to every spiritual virtue. If you were naturally quick-tempered before salvation, you might have initially seen patience as a singular gift, a "salvation in itself" that would fix everything. It might have sustained you for a couple of years, but eventually, it 'fizzled out.' Your self-effort and the initial grace-as-a-gift proved to be temporary.

God performs this continuous work—this deep process of removing and replacing—in the lives of all His children. He takes away not only the distractions of the world but, most profoundly, the *spiritual things* we lean on. Before we were saved, the things of this world naturally took the place that belongs to Christ. Now that we are saved, we can be tempted to replace that worldly focus with spiritual **things**—good qualities, experiences, or ministries—that also subtly begin to occupy Christ's central place.

But God is on a mission to show us a new, breathtaking reality: **"Christ is my all."** He removes your personal patience, your self-generated love, your human power, your natural gentleness, and your self-wrought humility. He removes all of it so that your life is no longer supported by a collection of good *things*, but sustained by a living **Person**. We are patient, not because we have received a *power* to be patient, but because we have received a *Person*—Christ—who is patience itself. This is the truth for humility, gentleness, and every other virtue: it is not a power, but a Person.

This explains why God engages in a continuous process of **destroying and building**. He is daily dismantling our reliance on *things* so that He can daily build up **Christ** in our experience. In the past, you might have prayed for a gift or a power to solve a specific problem, like impatience or a lack of humility. You felt a problem was solved, only to move on to the next one, trying to tackle fractional problems one by one.

Here is a vital truth to hold onto: God must gently but firmly remove every thing that isn't Christ.

The encouraging news is that God is simplifying your entire spiritual life. He is taking away all those separate 'things' so that He can at once give you one all-encompassing **Person** who *is* simultaneously your humility, your patience, your gentleness, and your love. **Christ is all**, and this is the true essence of vibrant Christianity. God works relentlessly until not just our hearts, but the entire universe will confess that Christ is indeed everything. Today, His greatest desire is to work out this deep, settled confession in you: **Christ is all.**

Think about the profound difference this makes in how we relate to others. When ministering to someone struggling, we might instinctively exhort him, "You lack love, you must try to show more love to them next time." If he succeeds through sheer willpower, he has attained love as a mere *thing*, a behavioral adjustment. This results in what we might call a **behaving Christianity**—a life consisting of exhibiting certain correct behaviors through human effort: man is working, asking, expecting, believing, and succeeding in an outward act of love. In this scenario, love is only a *mark of behavior*.

This is a universe away from the experience of having **Love as Christ**. When love is Christ, it ceases to be a strained behavior of the human will and becomes a spontaneous **law of life**. It is no longer **I** who am working to love; it is **Christ** who loves through me. What a truly distinct and glorious Christian life this is, free from the exhaustion of self-effort!

"I have been crucified with Christ [in Him I have shared His crucifixion]**; it is no longer I who live, but Christ lives in me. The life I now live in the body I live by faith** [by adhering to, relying on, and completely trusting] **in the Son of God, who loved me and gave Himself up for me"**. (Galatians 2:20 AMP)

It's crucial to ask yourself: When you help someone, do they walk away equipped with a new spiritual *thing* or do they walk away with a deeper *revelation of Christ*? Many sincere believers are still occupied with 'the things' in Christianity—the virtues, the methods, the gifts—and have yet to know Christ as God's magnificent everything. God's grace is actively at work, stripping away all substitutes to reveal the only enduring, life-giving source: the Person of Jesus Christ. Your spiritual growth is not a task to be accomplished, but a Person to be continually discovered.

The Deeper Dive: Experiencing Christ as Your All

Let's explore what it truly means to move beyond simply knowing about Christ to genuinely knowing Christ in the practical, moment-by-moment reality of your life. This isn't about theological theory; it's about a transformation that touches your daily existence—your "things and affairs."

To know Christ in this deeper sense means recognizing Him as the very essence of your virtues. For instance, you move past striving to have patience and discover that Christ is your patience. You no longer try to muster love; you realize that Christ is your love. Others may discover that Christ has become their very humility. This level of knowing is the catalyst for a fundamental, dramatic, and liberating change in your life.

When this revelation dawns, you can confidently declare that there are no more separate "things" in your spiritual world. Your world, even your Christian walk, is entirely and beautifully summed up in Christ. You have no holiness outside of Him, and that's the good news. This doesn't mean you are unholy; it means your holiness is no longer a personal standard you struggle to meet. Instead, Christ is now your holiness. This immediate comprehension that "Christ is all" completely frees you from the exhausting effort of maintaining outward, self-generated matters. The entire path to spiritual maturity is wrapped up in this single pursuit: a living knowledge of Christ, not a matter of sheer willpower, endless prayer requests for things, or external encouragement.

This is a critical truth for our faith: lasting change is never sparked by mere exhortation or encouragement. While encouraging words can temporarily motivate a person to self-effort, true, effective transformation happens when God opens their spiritual eyes to know Christ. Our most sincere efforts may be repeated a hundred times without lasting result, until we see that Christ is the very solution we are seeking.

Consider the common struggle with Christian virtues. Many believers know Christ as their Lord who justifies them, but they still struggle with fear before God because they haven't experienced Christ as their righteousness. Likewise, many know Him as the Sanctifier, yet they constantly feel inadequate in holiness. Why? They chase holiness as a 'thing'—a goal to be achieved. They ask the Sanctifier to give them power to be holy. But as they rely on that 'power,' they inevitably hit a wall, discovering their personal inability to sustain it.

Their struggle is surmounted and their hearts are set free only after God opens their eyes to see that Christ is their holiness—not their sincere desire for holiness, and not even the power to be holy that He grants. Christ becomes holiness in them. This is the profound stability and assurance of the Christian life: we may lose power or fail in our actions, but we can never lose Christ. Our genuine holiness is settled, resting entirely on what He is to us, not on what we do. When we know Him as all, our most persistent problems are solved. The ultimate message is singular and powerful: Christ is all.

Here is a common point of confusion: many people know Christ as their Lord, but they don't yet know Him as their things and affairs. We often perceive Christ only in terms of His acts, which can be seen in the "-er" titles:

- **Savior**
- **Redeemer**
- **Sanctifier**
- **Justifier**

But God desires us to know Him in the deeper, more profound reality of the "-tion" titles:

- **Salvation**
- **Redemption**
- **Sanctification**
- **Justification**

To know Him as the "-er" is fundamental knowledge; to know Him as the "-tion"—the actual essence of the deed—is the further and deeper knowing.

The spiritual lives of many believers are cluttered with too many separate "things." The day we finally see that "He is", and that every one of our spiritual needs has been consolidated into a single, glorious Person, is the day God's eternal purpose is realized in us. As long as our sanctification, redemption, regeneration, power, grace, and gifts remain as separate objects that we seek, we are standing on the perimeter of Christianity. But when we see that these are not things, but the Lord Himself, we truly enter into God's eternal purpose. From that moment forward, it's always He, never things.

The "things" we labor to achieve by our own strength are, in a spiritual sense, dead. Once we realize this, those very "things" lose their power over us and find their true reality and vitality in the Person of Christ. My regeneration, for instance, is not a concept; it has a Personality. Christ, whom I possess, is a Person, not a thing. Every virtue and blessing I have carries His personality because the Lord is all. He leads us first to know Him, and then He leads us further into knowing Him as everything we need. In this, we are truly set free from the burden of our own self-life and the endless striving of the spiritual world.

We can testify that in our daily living, He is all.

- If I am patient today, it is not I who is patient, but **He who lives in me is patient.**
- If I love, it's not because I'm trying my best to love—the power isn't in me—but because there is **One who loves in me.**
- If I forgive, it's not due to my effort, generosity, or capacity; it is purely due to the **One who lives in me and always forgives.** He is my forgiveness.
- If I am humble, it's not because I'm suppressing pride or forcing a humble attitude; it is the **Person in me who so humbles.** Since He is my humility, I am consequently humble.

This is the beautiful **law of life**: Christ becoming our life as well as the essence of all our spiritual virtues.

Therefore, let us all sincerely ask God to open our eyes so that we might truly see this monumental reality. All of our human efforts, methods, and external 'things' will eventually fade away, but what remains is eternally **Christ**. May we live out this incredible truth every day and let **Christ be all** in our hearts right now.

Let us Pray!

Father,

We come before You with humility and gratitude, marveling at the depth of Your provision in Your Son, Jesus Christ.

We acknowledge that, often, we are content to know Him only by His acts, as the Savior who rescues us and the Justifier who declares our innocence. But today, with open hearts, we seek to go beyond.

We ask You, Father, to open our spiritual eyes so that we may see the monumental reality that Christ is much more than the One who performs a work: He is the very work itself.

May we perceive that He is not just our Savior, but our complete and ultimate Salvation. He is not just our Justifier, but our eternal Justification. He is, in fact, our Santification, our Redemption, and our Hope.

We surrender to You all our human efforts, our flawed methods, and the external "things" we incessantly seek. We know that all of this is temporary and has no efficacy. Help us to live with the rest and assurance that only the eternal Christ remains.

Amen.

7

The Cross

The Essential Key to Living by Christ's Life

Let's look at the purpose of the cross with absolute clarity and with an encouraging perspective. The Cross of Christ is not just the key to our salvation from sin; it is the daily operational key for our entire spiritual life. We can state it plainly: **If you are living life based on your own strength—your 'things'—you actually don't need the power of the cross.** But if you are committed to living by the Person of Christ, you will continually embrace the cross.

The cross is an all-encompassing force. Yes, it radically deals with our sin, cutting off everything that is overtly evil. However, in our spiritual journey, it goes deeper: **it inhibits our self-generated activity.** It's designed to curb our own actions and check our natural desire to perform, even our desire to do good.

This is where many sincere believers run into a profound difficulty. They genuinely want to do good, to be compassionate, and to serve others. Yet, they fail to realize that this self-produced "goodness" is just another *thing*—a spiritual product of their own natural energy. In God's eyes, the entire issue, the single substance, is **Christ Himself**. He is the *only* true good thing, the source of all life.

Think about this: If Christ, the very Life of your spirit, remains quiet, how can we dare to move on our own? We can easily launch into giving well-meaning advice or offering a flood of comforting words, but if He has not prompted it, we should restrain ourselves. Why? Because when we operate outside of His initiation, we find ourselves touching spiritual death. This is why you can help people, earn praise for your tender heart, and yet instantly feel a hollow, deflated weariness inside. The effort was genuine, but the source was empty.

This is the deeper power of the Cross: it doesn't just judge our evil; it judges our independent goodness. Any good we accomplish using our own skill, human strength, or religious willpower does not require the cross to be effective. The cross becomes essential only when we choose to step back and **allow the Lord to live through us**, making Him the source of our actions, our wisdom, and our everything.

We have to ask ourselves: If Christ makes no move, how can I? This is a daily surrender. We need to pray for deliverance from the tyranny of our own good works just as passionately as we pray for deliverance from our sins. For many, it is surprisingly easier to be delivered from blatant sin, which is clearly condemned, than it is to be delivered from our natural, yet self-centered, life. Why? Because our own "good works" are not rejected by the world, making them much harder to recognize and surrender. But the pathway to an effortless, fruitful life is to let the cross end our efforts, so that Christ's life may begin to flow.

Christ Alone

What is the fundamental, most liberating truth of our faith? It's a reality that often goes unrecognized: in the spiritual realm, **there is nothing but Christ.**

We often pursue what we call "spiritual virtues" as if they are separate, obtainable *things* we can collect on our journey. The same with our actions, our *work* for the Lord. We may want to do good but if He has not prompted it, we are operating outside of His initiation, and will find ourselves touching spiritual death. There are no spiritual commodities, just the simple and spontaneous expression of **Christ and Christ alone.**

When we first believed, a profound work happened in our lives: we were shown that we needed Christ, not religious *works*. We were saved by grace through faith in Him, not by our own diligent effort. This was the first, glorious revelation, which rightly obliterated our reliance on sin and self-justification.

Now, God is inviting us to an equally profound, second-phase revelation that brings even greater rest: what we need is Christ, not *things*.

If you are living life based on your own strength you actually don't need the power of the cross. But if you are committed to living by the Person of Christ, you will continually embrace the cross.

Just as we once had to let go of our sins—pride, jealousy, a quick temper—to receive Him, we must now allow the spiritual structure of our *self-styled holiness* to be "wrecked" so that Christ can truly become our all. We may be genuinely patient, sincerely humble, and exceptionally good in our conduct, earning high marks by human standards. But this is the crucial point: if these virtues originate from *us*—if they are the product of our striving, our religious discipline, or our character development *apart* from the continuous flow of His life—they are merely spiritual *things*.

And a spiritual *thing*, no matter how beautiful, is ultimately inert.

This deeper work of God is not about becoming a worse person; it's about becoming a **free** person. It's about being liberated from the crushing pressure of maintaining our own goodness. It's an invitation to stop building an impressive spiritual résumé and, instead, to simply understand, at the core of our being, that **Christ is our life and our all.** This is a victorious Christianity, vastly different from the performance-based faith the world often conceives.

Whoever Touches Christ Touches Life

This truth becomes wonderfully practical in our daily lives.

Let me share a simple experience that illustrates this principle clearly. There was a situation in a friend's life that required a visit—the "Christian duty" was clear, the compassionate act was obvious. So, I set out, motivated by a desire to be helpful and loving. Yet, the farther I walked, the heavier, and colder, my spirit became. All the spiritual joy drained away.

Why? Because I immediately realized my motivation had shifted. I was trying to *perform* an act of loving compassion *on my own steam*. The action itself was commendable and right—visiting a friend is a good thing!—but because **I** was doing it, it was a "thing" I manufactured, and I had instantly encountered spiritual death. The result of that self-initiated task would have been an *inward freeze*, an act of compassion without the *life* of Christ in it.

This is a vital lesson for us all: **When you touch Christ, you touch life; when you only touch conduct, you will encounter death.**

We need to let the Cross of Christ touch not just our behavior but also our motivation. Christianity isn't a complex inventory of good *items* you gather or do. You could compile every ounce of humility, patience, and good deeds on earth, and you still wouldn't have the reality of a Christian life, Christ would be missing.

The glorious simplicity is this: Everything Christ gives is, in reality, His very own Self.

- He doesn't just grant you **patience**; **He is your Patience** dwelling within you.
- He doesn't just provide **righteousness**; **He is your Righteousness** that makes you completely acceptable to God.
- He doesn't just offer you **life**; **He is your Life** flowing effortlessly through you.

When we live our lives before God and rely on the 'thing'—our own kindness, our own wisdom, our own efforts—we touch death because Christ is not the source. But the moment we reach out in simple faith and touch **Christ Himself**, we immediately encounter life—vibrant, eternal, abundant life, because **He Himself is Life**.

Freedom: Trading Striving for the Life of Christ

It's a deeply relatable experience for those of us who sincerely love God: we set out to serve Him, wanting to do *more* and live a life that truly honors Him. On the surface, our tasks are excellent, even requiring sacrifice, suffering, and giving our very best. We expect to feel alive, fulfilled, and blessed in this service.

Yet, many of us have faced a puzzling and painful contradiction. Despite our genuine dedication and good intentions, we sometimes feel completely drained, weakened, and strangely *reproved* on the inside. Instead of touching vibrant, spiritual life, we feel as though we've touched a chilling emptiness—a kind of spiritual death. Our internal conscience, which we assume should only sting us when we've sinned, surprisingly censures us when we're trying to do something *good*.

When you touch Christ, you touch life; when you only touch conduct, you will encounter death.

When did we go wrong? The error wasn't in the *action* itself, but in the *source*. It happened the moment we conceived the idea that the strength, wisdom, and energy for serving God must originate *from us*. We leaned on our capacity to manufacture a "good work," and in that self-driven effort, we instantly encountered spiritual depletion. It is truly an eye-opening and sobering reality: sometimes, we receive a sharper, more painful inner correction from the Lord for our self-initiated *good* than we do for our outright failure, because the former masquerades as His will when it is rooted in self.

This is why the principle before God is not the **Tree of the Knowledge of Good and Evil**, but the **Tree of Life**.

The Tree of the Knowledge of Good and Evil represents any action—even a moral, religious, or commendable one—that is performed based on our own assessment, strength, or ability. Its fruit, no matter how "good" it tastes to our ego, leads to spiritual death because it is a life lived *apart* from Christ as the only Source. It's an inadequate foundation because the entire issue of Christianity is not a question of morality or performance; **it is a matter of life itself.**

The wonderful news is that the **Tree of Life is living**!

This is our liberating truth: God's deepest desire is for you to step off the treadmill of self-effort. He is not just our Judge when we sin; the One who lives in us, the Holy Spirit, is also our tender Guide who will redirect us when we attempt to do His work through our own strength. He chides us, not to condemn, but to rescue us from the weakness and emptiness of self-generated goodness.

Your job is not to strive to be good, but to simply **connect**—to abide in Christ, who is your life. Everything good, true, and life-giving flows only from Him. Every time you consciously choose to draw your motivation and strength from Christ, you touch life. This is the effortless, fruitful, and eternal way of God, where your spiritual service is no longer a draining duty, but a joyful overflow of the living Christ within you.

Spiritual "Things" are Limited, Christ is Limitless

What is the object of our most earnest spiritual pursuit? For many, it's the search for a *thing*—a specific virtue or spiritual quality that feels missing from their lives.

For example, there are countless sincere Christians who express a deep, almost desperate, longing for patience. They are often profoundly frustrated by their quick-tempered nature, genuinely wishing for an instant solution. Their underlying thought is, "If I could just *be* patient... if God would simply give me a 'dose of patience' to swallow, then everything would be well." They seek patience as if it were a spiritual prescription or a kind of emotional medicine.

The challenging reality of this mindset is that anything you can *count* or *acquire* will eventually run out. You might be able to maintain this "self-sourced patience" for a few days or even a week, but because it is merely a *thing*—a temporary product of human willpower—it has a time limit. Eventually, that emotional reserve shrivels up, and the patience completely disappears. If a virtue is only an *item* you possess, even if it was obtained through sincere prayer, it will be exhausted, and you'll find yourself back where you started.

In His boundless grace, God is compassionate, and for a short season, He may accommodate the temporary need and "foolishness" of His children by answering prayers for these specific *things*. He helps us in our initial sincerity. However, He will not permit this condition to be indefinitely prolonged. Why?

The glorious, liberating reason is this: In God's ultimate plan and Word, **there is no separate "thing" apart from Christ—Christ is all in all.**

God will not allow patience, humility, or even love to exist on this earth as a self-sustaining *thing* because He intends to redirect our attention from the gift to the Giver. As we leave our self-sustaining *things* at the cross, for they are dead, He will reveal to us that **Christ is Patience**, **Christ is Humility**, and **Christ is Love**. It is the Person of Christ, not an impersonal item or a spiritual commodity acquired.

When our relationship with the Lord is truly "normalized"—when we stop seeking spiritual traits as separate items and recognize that Christ Himself is the source—we will find that all our personal problems are effortlessly resolved. It is never fundamentally a question of patience, character, or any other quality. **It is entirely a matter of Christ.**

As soon as our reliance on Christ is fully restored to the dynamic reality God designed, our multitude of problems will be duly resolved. The entire, all-encompassing question of our Christian life, victory, and character is Christ, not a collection of things. Rest in Him, for He is all you need.

Let us Pray!

Father God, I come before you now to wholeheartedly accept and embrace the profound reality of the cross of Christ. I receive the glorious truth that my life's journey is centered on your will to sum up all things in Jesus.

I confess that the work of the cross is not merely a historical event I remember, but a daily event I embrace, and I welcome its continuous, transforming power in me. I accept that at the cross, Christ declared, "It is finished," and it is in that finished work that my real life begins and finds its conclusion.

I no longer look to my own striving, but to His ultimate sacrifice, seeing there the very heart of your love, saving grace, and the key to the deepest revelation of His identity.

I embrace the truth that I have already died to my old life, and I surrender my old self, knowing my new, real life is hidden securely with Christ.

I thank you that Christ is the very source of my strength and purpose, and I rest confidently in the truth that He is my Sanctification, not a process, but a Person being lived out through me. I declare that I possess nothing but Christ, and in Him, I have everything.

I choose to abide in the liberating truth of the cross, where my life starts and ends.

Amen!

8

We Must Know Christ

The grand, singular truth at the heart of our walk with God is this: Every single issue, every challenge, and every victory revolves around one magnificent proposition—**the profound, personal knowledge of Jesus Christ.**

What does it truly mean to "know Christ"? It's far more than agreeing to a set of facts or having a correct theology. It is an **active, substantial, and utterly personal** experience. For some, they know Him as their boundless love; for others, they know Him as their perfect humility, their unending patience, or their unshakable peace. The measure of our spiritual life is precisely the measure to which we have discovered Christ to be the embodiment of all these necessary "things." This—and this alone—is the proper, vital knowledge of our Savior.

To know Him is to perceive Him not as a distant helper, but as **our living reality**. He is this "thing" for us, and He is that "thing" for us.

Think about a moment of genuine, transforming testimony. Someone who once felt utterly consumed by inner uncleanliness—whose thoughts, heart, and habits were a mess—can now stand up and declare: "I thank God, Christ has become my cleanness." It wasn't a sudden surge of willpower or a self-help program that fixed them. It was a moment of deep spiritual revelation that showed them: This cleanness is not a thing I possess; it is Christ Himself dwelling in me. This is the secret of Christianity: Christ is not a passive Guest; He is the Life who, by His presence, brings every spiritual virtue *with* Him. It's not about what belongs to your natural self; it's about what He brings in.

Crucial Distinction: Life vs. Death in Our Efforts

With this powerful truth in mind, we must look at our own spiritual life with honest eyes. I must state this plainly and with deep love: a child of God whose spiritual eyes have not yet been opened to see Christ as their *things*—as their very life-source for everything—is, in a profound sense, limited in their usefulness to God. Why? Because what they have left are simply their own good *works* and human *effort*.

Every single issue, every challenge, and every victory revolves around one magnificent proposition—the profound, personal knowledge of Jesus Christ.

You may pray earnestly and receive momentary grace from God, but if the final result is merely a "thing"—a temporary feeling of peace or a short burst of patience—it is destined to be fleeting and will carry little if any eternal spiritual value before God. We must face the sad reality that much of the grace people receive today is experienced as an *object*, a temporary fix.

However, a beautiful, victorious difference exists. Some believers receive grace with a **Personality**: their grace is not an abstract concept, but is the very **Son of God**. I long for the day you can declare to God with joyful confidence: "Father, I thank and praise You, because the grace I have received is not a feeling or a formula; my grace is a Person, having a Personality—**it is Christ.**"

The moment you see this difference, you can instantly distinguish **life from death**. Sadly, many sincere Christians are only able to discern between *good and evil*; they cannot differentiate between **life and death**. They fail to see that *everything* in the spiritual economy is contained in Christ. He is both the end goal and the means to achieve it. In the authentic, vibrant spiritual realm, there is no "thing" and no "affair," **there is only Christ.**

The Spiritual Touch of Death in "Good" Things

Once God truly opens your eyes to this reality, you become spiritually discerning. You start to recognize *things*—self-generated virtues—whenever you encounter them. This may sound strange at first, yet it is profoundly factual and liberating.

You may meet a person who is exceptionally patient, gentle, humble, loving, and generous. They are a model of virtue! Yet, to one whose eyes have been opened, that person is merely "full of things." Just as you can easily tell the difference between a coat and the person wearing it, you can now differentiate a religious *trait* from the indwelling *Christ*.

The critical and challenging truth is this: **Whatever belongs to "things" is dead within and produces death without.**

If a person operates from self-generated goodness, they may be very nice, but their influence is limited to the realm of simple human good and evil; it has no true, transforming spiritual effect. A person who is naturally good-natured, enduring, and loving may please you immensely, but if these characteristics are only traits of their *flesh*, they will, surprisingly, arouse a faint but unmistakable sense of **death** within you. Your spirit, being alive in Christ, cannot embrace a dead work, and an internal resistance will well up.

We have all felt this. Sometimes in a prayer meeting, a prayer is so full of the life of Christ that you spontaneously shout, "Amen!" because your spirit has been deeply touched by Life. But another prayer, though eloquent and earnest, leaves you with a chilling emptiness. You sense the desire for it to end, because the prayer feels like an extension of their personality— a "thing" of self-effort that carries the touch of death. A thing of man-made effort produces spiritual death not only in the person doing it but also in those around them, for there is absolutely no spiritual worth in what is done by man alone.

Christ Is Our Victory: The End of Our Works

Since this is the situation—since anything from our own effort carries the "touch of death"—we are led to the only viable path before God: **to wait on Him and to cease from our own works.**

As we are truly led forward by the Holy Spirit, we will make an astonishing discovery: **God hates our self-initiated works**

as much as He hates our sins. To those who commit sins, the wages is death. To those who rely on their own religious performance, they cannot be saved from their own self-life. God utterly rejects our works just as He repudiates our sins.

He accepts one thing only, and that is His Son, Jesus Christ. It is Christ who becomes all things to us. This is the great relief and the ultimate victory! It is not "I trying to be humble," but He humbling Himself in me. It is not "I struggling to love," but He loving instead. He doesn't just *give* me power; He Himself is my Power.

To those that just got saved, please grasp this as early as possible! **When you are delivered from the pursuit of spiritual *things*, you will finally touch the Lord Himself.** The longer you live in the "heap of things," the harder it becomes to break free. It may take God, in His deep love, putting you through a painful process of breaking and revealing your own limitations to take away these self-made items, so that you are finally desperate enough to receive Christ as your all.

He accepts one thing only, and that is His Son, Jesus Christ. It is Christ who becomes all things to us. This is the great relief and the ultimate victory!

We anticipate the glorious day when all things—in heaven and on earth—shall be summed up in Christ. But let me challenge you today: How can you expect Christ to be all on that future day if you do not know Him as your all today? Even now, Christ is ready to be all our things. God has given His very own Son to us; He has given *Himself* to us. Therefore, Christ must be our all-in-all today. There is no division between Christ and spiritual things. Nothing is spiritual, **only Christ is.** He is all, and He is in all.

May this reality begin to powerfully evidence itself in your life now. Declare today that Christ is all and that He is in all: "He is in my patience! He is in my gentleness! He is in my love! For He is all!" We look forward with joy to that day when the Son of God is manifested to be all and in all, but the lessons we learn today are the very experience that prepares us for that full manifestation. God bless you as you rest and live in Him.

Let us Pray!

Our Father, we humbly approach Your presence, acknowledging our deep and constant need for Your grace. Lord, we confess that our spiritual vision is often clouded. We look at the world around us, and the "things" of this life feel intensely real and urgent. Yet, in the same moment, You, Christ Jesus, the very center of all reality, can seem distant and abstract. We often know the concepts of Christianity, but we fail to truly know You.

We pray with all sincerity, Lord, open our eyes! Grant us a divine vision that pierces the veil of the material and the merely religious. We ask that Christ would become so vividly real to us that everything else—all the striving, all the self-effort, all the spiritual clutter— would fade into the background. Let the fleeting things of this life lose their grip, and let Your abundant, vibrant life fill every corner of our being.

Father, we sincerely pray for deliverance from the tyranny of "countable things." Free us from the mindset that sees spiritual growth as virtues we must acquire. Instead of chasing after abstract qualities teach us to simply know the Lord who is a Person. May You, the Living Christ, become the all-encompassing reality that defines and replaces all the "countable things" we mistakenly pursue. Establish a connection so deep that people don't see our effort, but they see Christ in us.

Help us to grasp the magnificent contrast between a life rooted in Your Son and one based on our own efforts. We recognize that true growth requires the breaking of our self-sufficiency. We yield to this necessary process.

Help us to grasp the magnificent contrast between a life rooted in Your Son and one based on our own efforts. Cause us to understand how different the way of true Christian living is from any mere imitation or false substitute. We recognize that true growth requires the breaking of our self-sufficiency. We yield to this necessary process.

Do not allow us to deceive ourselves into believing we are full of life when we are merely full of our own dead "things."

We ask for Your powerful touch, Lord. Take firm, permanent residence within us, so that from the deepest core of our being outward, it is Christ and Christ alone.

Finally, we pray a blessing over this message and every word spoken, that You would use it to bring countless hearts back to the singular, all-sufficient Person of Your Son. Where human weakness fails and our own words fall short, may Your Holy Spirit speak. We ask that You would redeem our foolishness and use this moment to bring glory to Your Name. May this be a day of deep spiritual exposure for many, where every falsehood is uncovered, and You, Christ Jesus, are clearly distinguished from all man-made substitutes. Bless Your own Word and glorify Your Name, for in the name of the Lord Jesus, we believe and pray.

Amen!

About the Author

Helber's journey began with a profound, life-altering realization: God was personally pursuing him, even though he was not pursuing God. This discovery led him to the liberating truth that the Christian faith is not a religious checklist, but a deepening, intimate relationship with the living person of Jesus Christ. In his walk with Jesus, he found a hope and freedom that increases daily—not a momentary spark that dims with time. His passion is to share that Christ is not just a part of life, but the absolute and total provision in whom all truth and purpose eternally reside. He and his wife currently live in Northern California, where they serve in their local church.

For more information, please email us at hgsouza@freetosetfree.com.

www.ingramcontent.com/pod-product-compliance
Lightning Source LLC
Chambersburg PA
CBHW071443130726
47997CB00006B/2210